FORGIVENESS

FORGIVENESS

A Memoir

Chiquis Rivera

WITH **María García**

WITHDRAWN

ATRIA PAPERBACK

NEW YORK   LONDON   TORONTO   SYDNEY   NEW DELHI

ATRIA PAPERBACK

An Imprint of Simon & Schuster, Inc.
1230 Avenue of the Americas
New York, NY 10020

First Atria Paperback edition April 2015

ATRIA PAPERBACK and colophon are trademarks of Simon & Schuster, Inc.

For information about special discounts for bulk purchases,
please contact Simon & Schuster Special Sales at 1-866-506-1949
or business@simonandschuster.com.

The Simon & Schuster Speakers Bureau can bring authors
to your live event. For more information or to book an event
contact the Simon & Schuster Speakers Bureau at 1-866-248-3049
or visit our website at www.simonspeakers.com.

Interior design by Esther Paradelo

Manufactured in the United States of America

10   9   8   7   6   5   4   3

Library of Congress Cataloging-in-Publication Data

Rivera, Chiquis, author.
    Forgiveness : a memoir / Chiquis Rivera.—First Atria paperback edition.
        pages cm
    1. Rivera, Chiquis. 2. Rivera, Jenni. 3. Singers—United States—Biography.
I. Fitz, Ezra E., translator. II. Title.
    ML420.R64A3 2015b
    782.42164092—dc23
    [B]
                                        2014049246

ISBN 978-1-5011-0481-7
ISBN 978-1-5011-0483-1 (ebook)

I dedicate this book, with all my heart, to my great love, God. You have never turned your back on me nor forsaken me, even when I deserved it. I can feel that I'm missing my mother or my father in this world, but I am never lacking in You.

A Guardian Angel for You

An angel watches over you
in everything you do.
The Lord has sent her down to earth
to guide and comfort you.

She'll see you through your sadness
and help you through your pain.
She understands the feelings
that words cannot explain.

This angel's a reminder
of God's amazing love —
A gift to fill your heart with hope
and strength from up above.

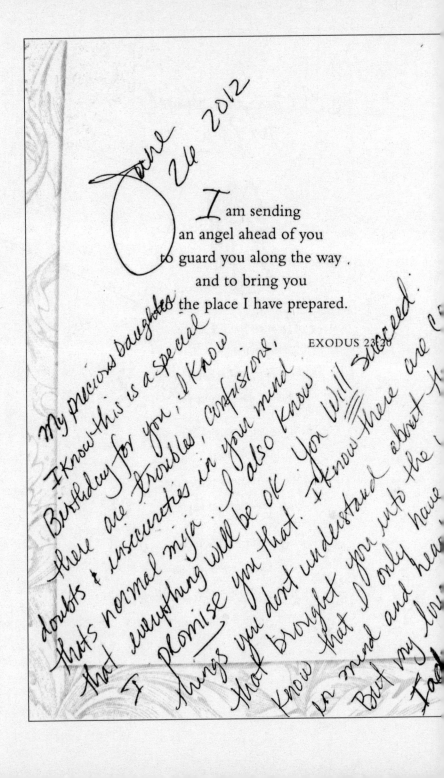

June 20 2012

I am sending
an angel ahead of you
to guard you along the way
and to bring you
the place I have prepared.

EXODUS 23:20

My precious daughter
I know this is a special
Birthday for you, I know
there are troubles, confusions,
doubts & insecurities in your mind
thats normal mija. I also know
that everything will be OK. You will succeed.
I promise you that. I know there are
things you dont understand about ti-
that brought you into the
know that I only have
in mind and hear
But my lov
Fad

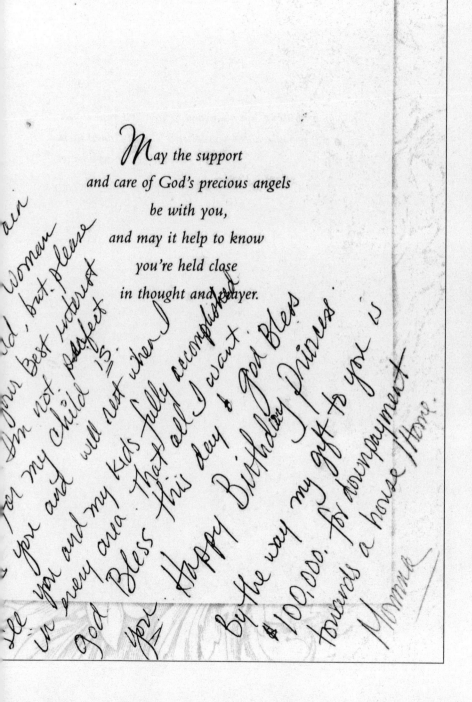

May the support
and care of God's precious angels
be with you,
and may it help to know
you're held close
in thought and prayer.

...ain woman ...d, but please ...your best interest. Am not perfect for my child 15. you and will not when I see you and my kids fully accomplished in every area. That all I want. God Bless this day & God Bless you. Happy Birthday Princess. By the way my gift to you is $100,000. for downpayment towards a house /Home.

Momma

You own everything that happened to you. Tell your stories.
If people wanted you to write warmly about them,
they should've behaved better.

—ANNE LAMOTT, *BIRD BY BIRD*

CONTENTS

CONTENTS

I lost my mother on October 2, 2012. Another date on my calendar. And there's no delete button to erase it from my heart.

My family, her fans and the whole world said good-bye to Jenni Rivera on December 9 of that same year, but I lost her first, on that strange Tuesday earlier in the fall. That was the moment when my pain and mourning began. The heaviest weight I've had to bear thus far.

I remember our final meeting down to the last detail. The clock showed it was nine in the morning. We'd be seeing each other soon in Long Beach, our sweet old Long Beach.

1.

BICYCLES AND GARAGES

I think it was winter, judging by the freezing wind hitting my cheeks. Though it's hard to be sure in Long Beach—with the mist blowing in off the Pacific, the mornings were always overcast and that chilly humidity soaked into your bones. What I do remember with perfect clarity is the bike: one of those cheap beach cruisers. I rode in the back, in the child seat, wrapped up like a tamale in my coat, my hat and I don't know how many sweaters, with my chubby cheeks getting flushed in the wind.

This is the first mental picture I have of my mother: pedaling hard, hands firmly gripping the handlebars, her dark, coffee-colored hair pulled back in a ponytail and her head held high. It was 1989. I had just turned three, she was eighteen and our car had just been stolen.

"It's okay, baby, we're almost there. Don't worry."

I remember how she would say that—"don't worry"—and somehow her words made it so I didn't feel the cold. We lurched on down the street, past the houses with their gardens in perfect rows and tangled bougainvillea on their porches. What could I have to fear, if my Super Momma was in charge?

The night before, I'd woken up to the sound of breaking glass. I slowly dragged myself over to the only window facing the alley, and there I saw, just a few feet away from me, two guys wearing Halloween masks getting into my mom's car. It was an old little clunker, and I can't even remember what color it was. Suddenly I heard the tires squealing, and the two shadows sped away.

Just then, my mother—who had been watching everything, right there at my side, motionless in the dark little room—hugged me tightly and took me back to bed. She didn't say a word, but from the look in her eyes, she was pissed. There were no signs of fear on her face; my mother never let me see her afraid. If I hadn't been there, things could have gotten very ugly for those punks. No doubt about it.

The next morning, my mom got up early and quickly pumped up the tires of her bike. In the blink of an eye, she had me securely strapped to the back seat, and we were on our way to school.

Back then, my mother, Dolores Janney Rivera, was just another kid who wasn't even dreaming about making it big and becoming famous. She'd temporarily separated from my father, José Trinidad Marín. Those were tough times, with lots of twists and turns. My momma, a top student at Long Beach Polytechnic High School, got pregnant with me when she was fifteen and effectively had to put all of her studies and plans for college on hold in order to face her new reality. My parents both felt pressured by their families and strong Latin tradition, which dictated that you must be married before you could have a child. My father, whom everyone called Trino, was twenty-one and felt trapped in a corner with no way out. He had gotten my mom pregnant and now his only option was to take care of her. Meanwhile, my mother had been kicked out of her house by her parents. Both came from Mexican immigrant families, workers who were trying to make the streets of Long Beach and Los Angeles their new home.

And there I was, in the middle of it all, in that garage facing the alley behind my uncle Gus's house, where my mother and I spent several months sleeping alone on a mattress on the floor. My mom was too proud to ask my grandmother to take us back. No way! She was going to take care of me in whatever way she could, even if it was in that dark little garage that was never intended to be set up as a guest room. Every night we ended up there, huddling under the covers. And my greatest joy was for the sun to come up in the morning, so we could get out of there. First, day care, and in the afternoon, to my grandma Rosa's house, where she would take care of me until my momma got off work.

Back then, Chay (as she had been affectionately nicknamed by her siblings) had two jobs: one at an office, and the other at a video store. Her days seemed endless, and mine did too, waiting at Grandma's house for her to come back for me.

When night fell, the mattress in the garage was there waiting for us. Next to it was the bicycle with the child seat firmly attached to the back.

And that—my first adventure on the back of that bike, the images of which I keep so clearly and so fondly preserved in my mind—is how I would picture my mother for the rest of my life, or rather, for the rest of her short but intense life: fearless, pedaling away, her head held high. With the steadying words "Don't worry, baby" always on her lips, which gave me more comfort than she could possibly have imagined.

That's how it begins: my story of great joys and challenges, of setbacks and successes and bitter pills to swallow, but, most importantly, my story is one of love and forgiveness. These are the experiences I want to share. Because if I've learned anything, it's that life is always our best teacher, and we'd better not cut any classes.

2.

THE SWAP MEET PRINCESS

The alarm rang at four, and the still-dark house already smelled of coffee being brewed.

My grandma Rosa woke me up. Like always, her hair and makeup were already done.

"Come on, *mija*, hurry up! We're about to leave."

Not without me! I'd never miss a Saturday at the swap meet, no way. I jumped out of bed and got dressed in a flash.

By that time we were living with my mother's parents again. My mom was pregnant for the second time

Her only option was to move the two of us back to the house on Gale Street, and accept her mother's help.

∞

My poor momma—this pregnancy was a real kick in the gut. She was still just a kid, 18 years old, and once again she was watching her dreams be cut short. Even so, she never stopped going to her night classes for business administration. Her life was basically work during the day, take care of me at night, study in the morning and now she was going to have another baby.

I remember my momma sitting on Abuelita Rosa's couch, her hair dark and short. She cried day and night. I think she cried the full nine months of the pregnancy. My mom didn't believe in abortion.

"I'm fine, baby, I'm fine," she said every time I went up to her to dry her tears.

She cried until she gave birth to the most beautiful little baby girl in the world. Even today I'm convinced that Jacquelin came to heal that sadness and bring a light into all of our lives. Mine included. That was late in 1989, and I was obsessed with the idea of having a little sister to play with. My mom was so overjoyed to hold Jacqie in her arms that she got her mischievous little laugh back, along with her joy for life, even though the turmoil with my dad would continue.

And with that turmoil, the coming and going. We spent the next three years bouncing around from house to house and then back again with my grandparents. Every time my parents reconciled, they looked for someplace to live. And every time they fought, my mom, Jacqie and I went back to Don Pedro and Doña Rosa. I have to admit, I secretly wished they would fight because it meant that we would be going back to the house on Gale Street. Later it would be *"la casa de* Ellis Street," after my grandparents moved across town, but always in Long Beach, and always full of love and unforgettable smells.

Ahhhh! I close my eyes and I can still breathe in the smell of Pine-Sol, so strong that it almost choked me. I have yet to meet a woman who mops the floors more than my grandma. I swear, she could go into the *Guinness Book of World Records* with curlers in her hair, her mop in one hand and a cigarette in the other. She would smoke day and night, like one of the old Hollywood actresses, until she became a Christian and the cigarettes went out the window.

But more than Pine-Sol and cigarette smoke, the one scent that flavored my childhood was the smell of beans. Every day, without exception, my grandma would put on a pot of beans to cook, so that they would be ready by the time my grandfather got home. My Abuelito Pedro would sit there, alone in the kitchen, in front of a massive plate of such exquisite deliciousness, and devour the entire thing down with his *queso fresco*, tortillas. I think that's why I'm a proud "beaner" to this day. Beans with *queso fresco*, tortillas, and a giant crunchy jalapeño—if I had my choice, that would be my last meal.

And the sun! I remember it would just pour in through the front windows. Grandma Rosa really knew how to fill a room with light and love. I didn't find those sorts of feelings in the other places I lived. I spent the happiest moments of my life there with my mom and my relatives in the houses on Gale and Ellis streets.

And it wasn't just the Rivera home that was magical. Those neighborhood streets and the people who lived there also had their charms. At least for me.

Those neighborhoods were a melting pot of Mexican and African-American families, living side by side, though never mixing. *Mexicanos y morenitos*, as we said. Or Brown and Black, as they say. When it came to the Mexicans, some of them had just arrived in this country, while others, like us, had already started families here. They called us *pochos*, because supposedly we spoke bad English and bad Spanish as well. But that wasn't true for the Riveras! It was a rule in the Rivera house to only speak Spanish, and when we didn't Grandpa Pedro would give us a light smack on the back of the head. In the house, we only listened to Mexican music, and we watched TV in Spanish the whole damn day. My mom also made sure that we had a sense of our Mexican roots. Even though my mother and I were both born in the U.S., it was important to her that my Spanish be as good as my English, especially when it came to cursing people out. She insisted that we not use sayings like "Go to hell, asshole." It was always *"Vete a la chingada, pendejo"* in our household.

It was truly remarkable how well my momma could both speak and write Spanish. And then there's me, who didn't learn a word of English until kindergarten. But as the years went by, the streets and my friends ended up winning the battle against my grandpa and his traditional Spanish, and we started incorporating a bit of the famous Spanglish. But just a little! That's what you do when you're a girl from "Long Bishhh."

"Don't be out wandering the streets!" my grandma would yell at me as I walked out of the house.

Too late. I had already slammed the door behind me and was heading from house to house, looking for other girls in the neighborhood. I couldn't help it. I'd felt the call of the street. I loved to invite myself over to a friend's house for dinner, so I could watch how their families behaved. I wanted to see whether they were like us, the Riveras, who were always yelling, singing and cracking jokes. I wanted to compare the other moms to my own and see if they were as hardworking as my momma.

Those were the days of near total perfection that God had granted me, before I had to live with the destiny that He had in store for me.

My grandma would pick me up from school, and together we'd hop on the bus heading down Long Beach Boulevard. Hand in hand, we'd enter Robinsons-May, her favorite store, or the now-defunct Montgomery Ward, where we would spend hours just looking and browsing.

"If you behave yourself while I pick out a blouse, I'll give you a *cuora*," she said, offering a kind little bribe.

I'd get excited. "Twenty-five cents!"

My grandma loved to go shopping, and she was always perfectly made up with fresh-from-the-salon hair. So it's obvious where I inherited my love for going from store to store. I had a great teacher! My mom, on the other hand, hated it. Even when she was making thousands and thousands of dollars, dragging her to the mall was a serious ordeal.

Back on the bus, Grandma Rosa would tell me countless stories about the Rivera family.

My grandpa, Don Pedro, moved here from Sonora, Mexico, back in the sixties. He quickly earned some money working in the fields or at gas stations. Once he made enough money, he sent for my grandmother and my uncles Pedro and Gustavo, who were still young at the time, to join him in the U.S. My mom was the first one to be born in California, but she always jokingly brags that she was "born in the USA, *pero hecha en México*." According to my grandma, she crossed the border with my momma in her belly.

"I'm not sure whether we made her in La Barca, Jalisco or Caléxico, *mija*," she'd say with a mischievous grin.

Then came my tíos: Lupe, Juan, and Rosie. Rosie quickly became known as "baby doll," and was my mom's first little toy, so to speak.

By the time Rosie was born, Pedro—Tío Pete—was married to Tía Ramona and they lived in a separate house. They didn't have any children yet. I was the first and only grandchild—born four years after Rosie—until they gave birth to my cousin Petey two years after my arrival. At this time they still hadn't given their lives over to God. Years later, Tío Pete would find his true passion, becoming the pastor of his own church.

Tío Gustavo and his wife gave birth to my cousin Karina the same year Petey was born. Tío Gus's calling was photography: he had a small business working as a photographer for weddings and *quinceañeras*.

Even though he was already married to María, Tío Lupe lived with us in that crazy, fun house with my grandparents, which made it that much better to go back there. He worked at Taco Bell, and I remember running to the door when he got home from work to see how many tacos he had brought me, all wrapped up in a paper bag—now that's the life!

Tío Juan was still a teenager, and was always running around causing trouble. He was very friendly and very flirtatious. He was always getting into something at school, and falling for every girl on the block, but I was his true princess. As time went on, Tío Juan became my protector, my guardian, the older brother I never had.

And finally there was my tía Rosie. Even though she looked more like my sister, my aunt was always a bit standoffish with me. She never let me touch her dolls, and wouldn't let me climb in her bed. I wondered whether it was because I was so little, and play-ing with kids can be a pain, but maybe she was a little bit jealous, because I stole all of her beloved Chay's attention away from her.

I was just dying to be her best friend. I constantly sought out her approval for everything I did, but she'd usually just yell, "Get outta my room!"

Many years later, I found out the real reason for her constant anger. Her agonizing torment—the same one that I would have to deal with years later—had already started by then. That house on Gale Street, which was a haven for me, was also the dungeon where my poor tía Rosie had her innocence stolen from her. But I'll tell you more about that later.

For now, let's talk about the swap meet. "*Mija*, your hair is a mess. Go comb it. You don't want people to see you looking like that!" My grandma was rushing me. We had to be in Paramount before sunrise. That was the best way to welcome in a new day.

I went into the bathroom that reeked of my grandpa's cologne and combed my hair as fast as I could. I was about five and had not yet adopted my grandpa's meticulous grooming habits.

My grandpa always liked to look sharp. He always kept himself in shape, well maintained and smelling good, regardless of whether he was going to work at a factory, meeting someone at a bar or going to one of the many little shops he opened up all over the place. But his one true passion—which we all ended up inheriting—was music. Don Pedro sang every chance he got, at parties and open-mike nights, and even in the shower. This passion eventually manifested itself in the formation of Cintas Acuario, his own label. My grandpa would record local musicians using his garage as a studio, and then, with the help of my mom and all my aunts and uncles, they'd dub the master tape. Back in the crazy eighties, it was all about cassette tapes, which is what led us to the swap meet, where we would sell those cassettes.

∞

"Hurry up and get in!" my grandma called from the front seat of their old green van, while my grandpa waited patiently behind the wheel. That old green van plays so prominently in my childhood. It is where we stored all of our stuff to set up our *puesto* and it is where I would go to take naps when I got tired, inhaling the smell of gasoline fumes as I slept.

That morning, all their merchandise had already been packed into the van. All that was missing was me. In twenty minutes, we'd be in the happiest place on earth: the Paramount Swap Meet.

"*Abuelita*, you didn't forget the hard-boiled eggs, did you?"

I wanted to make sure I wouldn't have to go without my favorite lunch. Those eggs made up the entirety of my menu, and I'd eat them so fast I'd almost choke.

We pulled into the massive, still-empty lot on Paramount Boulevard just as the first rays of the morning sun were stretching across the horizon. We quickly set up our blue tent before the big crowd started to arrive. I still remember the smell of that plastic tarp, which always fascinated me.

Then we started to set up the folding tables and organized the tapes for sale: some were new, some were used, some were pirated and others were by artists recorded by my grandpa.

My grandpa—always thinking like the music businessman that he was—would put a cup in front of the tables, and as soon as the crowd started to rush in, my grandma made me get up to dance and sing.

"Shake it, *mi* Chiquis! Shake it!"

Between chuckles and words of encouragement, people would toss coins into the cup. Encouraged by such a resounding response, I sang the lyrics to the music that all Mexicans carry in their backpacks when they make the move to the North: Los Razos, Saúl Viera, and Ezequiel Peña. And, of course, I also danced to the beat of the artists whom my grandpa represented in the hopes of making more money: artists like Chalino Sánchez, El Lobito de Sinaloa, Las Voces del Ranchero and his favorite, Graciela Beltrán. And then, of course, when Tío Lupe started singing, we'd play him constantly, blasting those beat-up speakers to death. My mom never managed to perform there on the swap meet stage. Her songs would hit the airwaves a little later, when I was a teenager and had swapped out those magical Saturdays there for time with my friends.

Whether he realized it or not, my grandpa Pedro, with the

stubbornness and tenacity of a great small businessman, was writing history. Decades later, he would be recognized as one of the pioneering stars of the swap meet. Radio broadcasters and major record label executives would walk past booths like his, looking to discover the hot new artists spreading throughout the community.

That day, we moved a lot of merchandise, and my cup was filled with clinking coins. My grandpa, who would disappear for hours at a time, looking into a thousand different business ventures, got back just in time to help us take down the tent and clean up the mess. When it was time to pack up and leave, I'd run to the food truck selling sweet breads and buy one for myself with my hard-earned money, along with a cup of hot chocolate. Then I'd hop back in the green van, completely happy with my life and my *bolillo* and *chocolate caliente.*

I remember that day in particular because after we got home and unloaded everything, I went to play soccer in front of the garage. And with one swift kick, I sent the damn ball straight under the green van. It was stuck. But then, a tall, slim man dressed in clean jeans, an ostrich belt and ostrich cowboy boots suddenly appeared.

"Here, hold this," he said, handing me his *tejana* before diving under the old van. "Here you go, kiddo. Here's your ball," he said. He didn't smile, but there was a kind look in his eyes. He seemed very quiet and serious, but I wasn't afraid.

That's the first memory I have of Chalino Sánchez. This was around the time when the calming, balladic *corridos* that became his style were starting to get airplay.

Along with Chalino's arrival there at my grandparents' house came the arrival of my first love: a platonic love, of course, but a love just the same. And, to this day, I'm still a bit embarrassed to admit that Adán Sánchez, son of the great Chalino, was the first boy who ever caught my eye. And damn, he was so cute.

Adán was also really smart. He didn't seem like all the other kids. He had a certain swag to him that I liked. He liked playing soccer and baseball with my uncles and doing other stuff that boys do, but at the same time he was gentle and super nice. I was seven and he was eight. I only dared to look at him from a distance.

But that was one serious crush! Three years later, when we were living on Fifty-Fifth Street, Adán's mother, Marisela, would often come and visit us. She'd been a widow ever since Chalino was brutally murdered in his hometown of Sinaloa. But, of course, his legend would grow even more after he was murdered, just two short years after I met him there in my driveway.

The glory of an artist goes beyond death: this is the strange and sad phenomenon to which the Chalino family and mine are witnesses.

But back then, Momma was on her own as well as Marisela, since my momma had recently separated from my father. The two quickly became friends. They'd go dancing from time to time, and somehow the best plan they could come up with was to leave Tío Juan in charge of all the kids. He was crazy! The house would turn into a party, and Jacqie, Adán and I would play until we dropped. One of those afternoons, Adán asked me if I'd be his girlfriend. I was jumping for joy!

He was my first sweaty-palmed boyfriend. We never even got to the first kiss, but how cute was that? He told everyone we were an item, and our moms would just laugh. They thought it was funny.

As we grew, Adán became a little too cool to be playing those dating games. That handsome young man was getting more and more serious about his own singing career, and his fame was starting to grow, just like it had for his late father. And my crush on him started to fade, but my affection for him never did. Somehow I continued to hang on to that platonic love during the time when an adult man robbed me of my innocence. Adán was my first prince charming, a perfect gentleman who never hurt me, never even forced me to hold hands, and who never knew—until we were both grown-ups—about what was happening in my life behind closed doors.

Years later, when he was at the height of his career, my dear Adán died in a car accident. Ironically, it was also in Sinaloa: the same city that had witnessed the death of his father. It was two weeks before his twentieth birthday.

We hadn't seen each other much during those last few years. Our families had grown apart, because of some problems between Marisela and my grandfather. But as destiny would have it, we bumped into each other at an event in Oxnard about a month before the accident. He was just about to go onstage, and thousands of fans were screaming his name. I didn't dare go up to him, so I just smiled at him from far away. But Adán walked over to me.

"Hey, Chiquis, how are you?"

I could tell that he was nervous. First he shook my hand, but then decided on a hug. It was one of those loving embraces between two people who never ceased being friends.

At that moment, everything—the noise and the crowd around us—disappeared. The clock stopped, and Adán looked at me with those eyes that could speak so well:

"*Lo siento* . . . I'm sorry we had to grow up so fast."

Bam! Back to reality. I didn't have time to answer him. The producer and the event coordinator grabbed him by the arm and dragged him up the stairs to the stage. He was on!

"Stay! I'll see you in a bit!" he shouted.

I nodded yes, but the truth is that I had to go. There was another commitment. And it was better that way. There are some stories best left unfinished.

A few weeks later, at his funeral, Marisela gave me another one of those long hugs that I'll never forget. The place was packed with fans and journalists, with love and pain alike. And I was foolish enough to go up to his casket. I still regret doing that. It would have been better if I had just left myself with the image of him standing there at the foot of the stage.

"Ay, Chiquis, my son always loved you," Marisela whispered into my ear with that tiny little voice that she had. Her arms didn't want to let me go from her embrace, and I didn't want to escape.

Marisela cried for Adán with a mother's tears, which are always the heaviest ones. His fans cried tears of devotion. I shed the tears of a girl. Like a third-grade schoolgirl. I cried for him like that first girlfriend who danced along to the songs of his father at the swap meet.

3.

THE HOUSE ON FIFTY-FIFTH STREET

I swear that during the early years of my life, we moved so many times that I can't even remember them all. It's hard to tell whether I was living in a trailer in Long Beach or that first sad, ugly little house we were renting in Compton when I lost my first tooth or when I started school. Maybe it was grandma's house? What a mess.

What I do remember is where we were when my brother Mikey came into this world: the house on Fifty-Fifth Street.

My mom and dad were back together and having one of their good streaks. They had just rented this house, not far from where my grandparents lived. That house on Fifty-Fifth Street was our first real home, though not for long.

My parents seemed happier than ever, and I even remember them talking and laughing together at night. They were feeling so good about things that they decided to have another baby. They were both hoping for *el chamaco*, the little man of the family.

And that's how Mikey came into our lives: the first planned baby of the three. They called him Trinidad Ángelo Marín. We started calling him Tongo right from the start, but when he grew up, he changed his name to Michael for other, more important reasons.

They say that babies are born with a loaf of bread under their arm. But our Tongo must have arrived with a pair of boxing gloves, because just a few weeks after he was born, the arguments and the pushing and shoving between Mom and Dad started up again in the kitchen.

By then, my mom had already finished her studies and was completely devoted to buying and selling houses, while still helping out at my grandpa's little record company.

My father was also working in real estate, but he spent more time with us at the house. He was the one who did the laundry, after which he would iron and fold it meticulously. In fact, he was the one who taught my mom how to clean and cook. Everything about him was neat and tidy, and all his stuff smelled like Zote, these bars of soap that were as big and hard as a brick.

My father liked Spanish rock. He didn't listen to *banda* or *corrido* music. He always wore a leather jacket and a white T-shirt, and his black hair was long and slicked back. He was sweet with us, and listened to us with a patience that was occasionally lacking in my mom. He talked to us like adults.

And that's how he spoke to me that afternoon in 1994.

Trino and Jenni—like oil and water—had just had their latest blowup that included a shove or two. They never hit one another in front of us.

It was getting dark, and my father sat me down on the sidewalk there in front of the house. He was wearing his leather jacket, which he usually did when he left the house upset.

"*Mija*," he said to me in Spanish, just as he always did. "It's not your fault, and it's not your brother or sister's fault either. Your

19

mom and I just aren't happy together anymore, which means we can't make you kids happy either. I know you'll understand."

"Yes, *Papá*," I replied, knowing that this was definitive.

"You have to take care of your siblings and help out your mom. I'll talk with Jenni about when you can come visit me."

I said "okay" to everything. He climbed into his tiny little car and drove off. Sitting there on the curb, I felt as if I'd just aged ten years. I had to grow up so damn fast! When the car turned the corner and disappeared down the street, I burst into tears.

I went back in the house, starting to feel afraid. Now, without my dad around, I was worried that Momma would get more strict with us.

But, much to my surprise, my mother was just waiting calmly there in the kitchen with a peaceful look in her eyes. She also spoke with me like an adult.

"How do you want to handle this? You're the oldest. Does it sound alright to you if you kids spend half the year with me and half with your father? And on the weekends, you could visit whichever one of us you're not staying with. I want your approval on this, Chiquis," she said seriously.

I told her I agreed, not knowing that the two of us had just sentenced me right then and there.

My father moved into an apartment with his sister Chuchi and her husband. My father set up some blue bunk beds in one of the rooms so that we could all fit. The first six months were spent with him and weekends with my mother. My momma was working extra hard at the realtor's office to pay off all the bills related to the house on Fifty-Fifth Street.

And there, in that room with the bunk beds, began the most horrific story of my life. A story that I have to tell exactly as it happened, because to leave anything out would mean that I'm ashamed, and that's not the case. For better or for worse, it's a part of who I am now. What happened to me happened, and I can't change that. And at this point in my life, it's clear that it was not my fault.

I'm telling this in a way I never have before, so that other victims can arm themselves with courage and stop hiding their pain. I won't be giving details because I'm trying to be morbid, but rather for the purposes of cleansing the soul and being transparent. Abuse is not something to be ashamed of. The most important thing is to face it and to move on.

Talking about it brings me a strange sense of peace, but this is only because I have forgiven those responsible.

4.

A DAY AT THE BEACH

It was a late summer Saturday. One of those days in Long Beach where you wake up to an overcast sunrise not knowing whether the sun will eventually come out and melt you alive or whether the skies will stay gray until the evening comes. In my mind, that day will forever be filled with clouds, and no matter how hard I try, I can't block it out, not even with the fog of passing time.

My father and my aunt decided to spend the morning at the beach so they wouldn't have to be locked up in the apartment with three kids. It was during the first month of our life as a divorced family, and we still weren't quite used to living with Dad for most of the week and spending so much time away from my mom. And we were also very young kids: Mikey was a ten-month-old baby, Jacqie was three and I had just turned eight.

We'd been at Redondo Beach, with its noisy seagulls and families, for less than an hour when a big wave smacked us hard and ripped Jacqie out of my hands. My baby sister was caught in a swirling undertow of foam and sand. "¡Papi, Papi!" I screamed in fear, but he wasn't even paying attention. He was too busy flirting with some girls. Luckily, one of my cousins reacted quickly, diving into the waves and pulling Jacqie out. She was bawling her eyes out, and so was I, from being so scared.

You could say that the party was over; that much was certain. With so much whimpering and sniveling, my father and my aunt quickly piled us all into the car and decided to take the drama home.

Once we got back to the little apartment where we lived, my father ordered me to take a bath. He insisted, over and over. "You get in the shower now!" he shouted. I wanted to take Jacqie with me because the poor thing had sand in her ears, but my father was adamant: "No, leave her in the living room. Go by yourself. Now."

I obeyed him and went into the bathroom. I was naked when he entered.

"Come here, *mija*, sit with me," he said. He was wearing nothing but his boxers, and sat down on the toilet seat.

I sat down next to him, but he picked me up and had me straddle his legs.

"You know I love you very much, *mija*. You know how much I do . . ." he started telling me. And as he was speaking softly to me, I started to feel some pressure on my private parts. A lot. I didn't understand any of it. Suddenly I cried out, "It hurts!" and I jumped down. It was then that I saw his penis, exposed through his boxers, but I still didn't understand what had just happened.

"Fine," he said, all nervous and upset. "Go clean up."

I obeyed and stood under the showerhead. My tears began to mingle with the water falling all over my body. "Nobody will know that I'm crying," I thought to myself, relieved. "The water will hide it all." But cry I did, out of pain and fear.

My father left the bathroom, but not long after that, he returned as if nothing had happened. He took off his boxers and got in the shower with me. And that's when the sweet talk began.

"I'm sorry, *mija*. Don't tell anyone. It won't happen again. I promise. Just don't tell anybody, and remember that I love you very much."

He lathered up, rinsed himself off and left in a flash.

That left me even more confused. *Whatever that was, it can't be that important*, I thought to myself, feeling very disoriented. I dried myself off, got dressed and went out to have dinner with my aunt and the rest of the family, all of whom were waiting for me in the dining room.

After such a gray, foreboding Saturday, my father avoided any contact with me for several weeks. I was afraid to even hug him when he came over, and I still didn't understand what had happened, but even at that age, my instincts were telling me that it was very wrong. That's when I started begging my mom:

"I want to come live with you. Please, Momma, I want to go to your house."

I kept pressing her without explaining why. I was terrified about what would happen if my mom found out. I didn't know why, but what I was feeling at that moment was pure horror. "*Mija*, it's normal. It's only been a few days. You'll get used to this house very soon," she said, looking to calm me. "Your aunt Chuchi takes good care of you, and I have so much work I have to do. You can come stay with me soon enough, *mi princesa*, I promise you." She was so focused on earning a few extra dollars so she could feed us and keep a roof over our heads that she couldn't possibly have imagined what was going on.

Meanwhile, the Devil always comes back for more. We slept together; my father, Jacqie and me in the bottom bunk, while Mikey slept by himself up top. Then one night, I woke up to find his fingers inside of me. I was petrified. Unable to move. I held my breath for as long as I could.

After that, I always made sure to sleep in the middle, so Jacqie wouldn't be next to him. I kept her to the side, up against the wall, so my father couldn't touch her. The instinct to protect her was born of some very profound place, though I didn't quite know why. I still didn't understand this new game my father was playing, but a little voice deep inside of me was telling me that it would be much more harmful to Jacqie than to me. And I would force myself to stay awake until I heard the slow, constant sound of my father's breathing. I was dying to fall asleep, to just drift off, but I had to wait for his eyes to shut if I was going to have anything close to a peaceful sleep. Either way, I knew that waking up wasn't going to be easy. If I couldn't sleep at night, I'd be nodding off all the next day.

The next morning, his only words were, "Don't tell anyone or I'll send you back to my family in Mexico and you'll never see your mother again." I was already scared of my other grandmother, his mother. She had never been good with me. I was terrified by the possibility of being separated from my mother and two younger siblings.

"Momma, I don't want to live at Papi's house anymore," I told my mom one day. "I don't like it there. They're mean to me. Please!" I begged her with all my soul.

I was so persistent that, after two months, my mother finally relented.

"Fine! If they don't want you there, then you're coming with me."

And that was it. From that point on, my father and his family started calling me a liar and accused me of making up stories about them being mean to me. To this day, that's all I am to them: the biggest liar in the world.

The agreement was changed. Starting then, we would be with

my mom from Monday through Friday, and then spend the weekend with my father. My mom was going a thousand miles an hour when it came to her job, and she needed the weekends to go out and sell houses. It was the perfect scenario for drawing the Devil out of a man who simply wouldn't give up. My father would take advantage of those weekends, exploiting my silence more and more while simultaneously becoming ever more aggressive. His growing boldness translated into longer, more fearsome and more painful sessions for me. All I remember is closing my eyes, tensing up my arms and thinking: *If I don't put up too much of a fight, then he'll be done with me sooner.*

From eight to twelve years of age, not a single Friday went by where I didn't wake up with a knot in the pit of my stomach. *Oh God!* I thought. *Today we have to go back to Dad's house.* It was so bad that to this day I still suffer from gastritis.

When we got to his house in the afternoon once school was out, he let us do whatever we wanted: he'd take us to movies, buy us candy and toys and let us stay up late at night. Everything that my mother considered off-limits. During the day he was an angel— a patient and attentive father—but when night fell, he became someone else entirely. That was when it happened: always when the lights were out.

To this day, I'm still terrified of the dark. I always leave a candle burning or a nightlight on so that I can sleep. Whenever I find myself surrounded by darkness, I feel like something terrible is about to happen.

You don't have a clear conscience, Chiquis. That's why you're afraid of the dark, my poor mother would joke every time I'd have to turn the light on before entering a room. *Do you think she knows?* I'd ask myself in a panic. But no, the truth is that she didn't know a thing, though she would be the one, some time later, who first put the pieces of the puzzle together. My mom was as clever as she was calculating. She would have made a great CIA agent, given the opportunity.

That's how I spent my ninth and tenth years: keeping that monstrous, despicable secret from my mother and from the world, deep down in the depths of my very core: Fridays. When I was in fifth grade I finally dared to confess it all to a friend of mine, the first and only friend I had during that time. We were in fifth grade and Valerie was my constant companion.

"You need to tell a grown-up. You have to," she told me. I remember the urgent look on her face after hearing the ugly details of my story.

"No, please," I begged her. "Don't tell your mom. Don't tell anybody. It's our secret. Please, *amiga*, please."

I pleaded with her so much that she never opened her mouth.

I felt just a bit of relief from knowing that someone else shared my sorrow, but it didn't help me much. The secret remained a secret. The fear was still fear. Fridays were still Fridays, and the Devil was still the Devil himself.

This was also the year when my suspicions that what my father was doing to me was filthy and wrong were confirmed. I, for all of my innocence, only sensed that it was strange, but then I started to hear the other girls at school laughing and joking about sex, saying that not only was it wrong, but sinful, as well. That's when I realized that my father was truly doing horrible things to me. It was disgusting! *Maybe I did the right thing by not telling anyone,* I thought, and with that I buried the thought even deeper into the back of my mind until I turned ten and discovered that I was not the only member of the family who was afraid of the dark, and the dirty, immoral games that came with it.

Tía Rosie was fourteen at the time. But she was more than just an aunt to me; she was like a sister. A big sister who was a bit testy and occasionally moody. And, like any little sister, I imitated her and did whatever I could to get her to like me. She was going through a rebellious, teenage phase, shutting herself up in her room and refusing to play with me. I even worried that she might be jealous of me. Aunt Rosie was my mom's favorite little darling, her beloved sister, until I was born—though, in truth, my mother never stopped loving and spoiling her. But the fact is that I soon discovered why my aunt always kept me away from her bedroom and her games.

"Yeah, your fucking dad is coming over. I hate that stupid bastard!" Rosie would yell at me. I never understood why she spoke to me with such rage in her voice, until one afternoon when (as my grandma says) the other shoe finally dropped: she was always acting strange around me because she couldn't stand my dad! She wasn't jealous of me; it was something that had to do with him.

That afternoon, when I saw her reading on the sofa bed, I took advantage of the opportunity to sit down next to her and start talking about random nonsense. Suddenly, out of nowhere, I said,

"I know why you hate my father so much."

"Huh? Why? *¿Por qué?*" she stammered. It was clear that my statement had thrown her off.

"Because he did the same things to you that he's doing to me," I said.

My aunt couldn't hide her shock, and the blood rushed out of her face. You could see the fear in her eyes. "How do you know?"

"I don't know, Tía Rosie. I can just feel it."

We told each other everything, our voices hushed for fear that someone might overhear us. We talked about the when and the where, but never any intimate details. It was incredibly difficult for both of us.

"With me, once I turned eleven, he started leaving me alone. What about you? Is he still doing it to you?" she asked me.

"No. It's been a few months now." And that was true. Just before my eleventh birthday, the abuse became less and less frequent, and eventually he stopped coming for me altogether when we were left alone.

"But, Chiquis, if he ever touches you again, you have to let me know so we can go tell your mom," Rosie demanded, her voice serious, though she was holding my hands with such care and concern that it killed off whatever distance had separated us for all those years.

"Okay, *tía*. Pinky promise."

And we hooked our pinky fingers to seal our secret.

From that moment onward, we became much closer friends. Rosie stopped giving me the cold shoulder all the time, let me into her room whenever I wanted, but we never again brought up the subject. Once was enough. At least, that's what we thought. But I never told her that just a few weeks after we talked about it, my father woke me up in the middle of the night yet again. And just like that, the fear and the pain came rushing back.

This lasted until I was twelve. Around this time I was just entering puberty, and some of my friends had already had their first periods. This gave me an idea. I asked Dora, my father's girlfriend, for a feminine napkin. By that point, she had been living with him for about a year, and had always been polite with me and—despite all the drama—she seemed to genuinely care about me.

"Ah, so it's already time?" she asked, intrigued.

"*Sí*," I replied, lying.

Of course, Dora went and told my father and, just as I expected, the midnight episodes stopped once again.

So from then on, every weekend that we'd visit him, I'd take it upon myself to steal a few napkins from Dora or my mother and put them on, just in case the Devil decided to rise again that night. God only knows, but thanks to that little invention of mine, my four-year-long nightmare had truly come to an end. Once and for all. Never again did my father touch so much as a hair on my head. That did not mean the fear was gone.

And the biggest bomb of all had yet to drop. The abuse might have been over, but the wounds were still very raw.

5.

PLAYING HOUSE

What I'm about to say here is something I haven't told anyone about since it happened twenty years ago. As I write this, I can feel my eyes glaze over and my throat tighten up. This is something I haven't confessed to any of the seemingly thousands of psychologists whom I saw during my teenage years, nor the doctors who treated me after the scandal with my father, nor the pastor of any church during my deepest spiritual crisis. I haven't even told my best friend Dayanna, whom I hope will forgive me. Nor have I confided in my best friend Gerald. Not even my current boyfriend, or any member of my family. I didn't even tell God when I would pray alone in silence! It's strange, and it's surprising even to myself that I can't quite explain why I've kept this secret buried so deeply.

The following pages will be the first place where I share this, after having checked first with my publisher and my publicist. Nobody else was involved. Together, we decided that the truth is less painful than keeping secrets. Both of them insisted that if I wasn't one hundred percent certain about this, I shouldn't talk about it.

But in the end, I decided to do it. Yes, I'm ready to talk about the other instance of sexual abuse that I suffered back when I was still a little girl.

Some might think that I'm doing this for publicity's sake, or to sell more copies of my book. But the truth is, I've decided to reveal this because I need to expose this secret that has been buried far deeper than any other in my entire life. I need to talk about it calmly, with no lights or cameras, and without any experts on the subject. I need to do this alone. I need to do it my way. And this book allows me to do that. These pages are mine alone, and I feel safe in them. You, by reading it, will provide my true therapy. You, in learning about this part of me that I've never let anyone see, will be better able to understand the rest of my story, and I will finally have the relief of knowing that this damn secret has finally seen the light of day. Because one thing that life has taught me is that wounds heal not in darkness, but in the sunlight.

My dear mother left this world without ever knowing this about me. She would learn about the abuse I suffered at the hands of my father, but never about this, and that brings on a flood of sadness. She passed away without telling me about the time she was raped by a group of strangers after leaving a bar. I had to read about that in her posthumous memoirs. And for my part, I was never able to tell her about this other case of abuse. Ironically, both our secrets ended up being published, revealed through ink on paper and never confessed in private, the way they should have been. I hope she can forgive me, wherever she may be, for not having told her. She never told me about the bitter spell she endured that night at the hands of those merciless thugs to protect me, and also because I'm sure it left her with a feeling of infinite sadness. I acted in the same way: I told no one in the hopes of avoiding further suffering, and because the sense of shame I felt was enormous.

I'm not sure why, but I felt more embarrassed about this secret than the highly publicized one about what happened to me at the hands of my own father. Perhaps it's because, in this case, the abuser was a woman.

This woman would come up to me and say, "Let's play house." I was nine, and just getting used to the games my father forced upon me.

It was just so confusing to be doubly victimized; I thought that playing house like that, hidden off in a corner, was normal. She would touch me, and she asked me to touch and stimulate her. *It's a woman . . . She won't hurt me like my dad.* That was my naïve and innocent reasoning at the time.

Gradually, these encounters—though they didn't happen very often—became, in my own little head, the worst form of torture. I didn't even mention them to Valerie, my friend who already knew about what was going on with my father. I was worried that she wouldn't want to be my friend anymore. I guess that's just how nine-year-old girls think.

The woman knew exactly what she was doing, but that didn't stop her. I slowly grew to resent her and to hate the time we spent playing house. Until one day she didn't ask me to play anymore and the afternoons spent in the corners disappeared, along with that abusive woman.

What didn't go away was the terrible sense of sexual confusion she instilled in me. With what I'd lived through—or rather, what I'd suffered—at the hands of my father, along with the suffering I was subjected to by her, well, it's needless to say that my sexuality has been a complete disaster for most of my life.

It should come as no surprise that years later I would question myself as to whether I was gay or straight, whether I could have a sexual relationship with a man or with a woman. Would I become so promiscuous that I wouldn't be able to maintain an exclusive relationship, or would I instead become completely celibate and alone? That's how terrified I was by even the thought of being touched, regardless of whether it was by a man or a woman.

In time, I was able to be physically intimate and to have stable and lasting relationships. But it wasn't easy. I have to admit that the road was full of twists and turns and some rough patches, which I'll be talking about here too.

I want other victims of abuse to read about my mistakes and fears and to see that it's possible to overcome them, as hollow as that phrase might sound. You can regain trust, if you put your trust in God. And you can learn to love again if you can learn how to forgive. If you can forgive the person who hurt you, the damage they did will start to fade, and it opens up space in your soul for good people to enter. But most of all, it will allow you to start loving yourself again. God and forgiveness, hand in hand, were my lifeline.

And I ask God for help even today. I'm nervous. I don't know what my family will think as they're reading this chapter. I hope they don't start asking me a lot of questions. I urge my fans and loved ones not to inquire further. I don't want to give out any more details. More about it would achieve nothing, and instead result only in more harm. My story must continue, and my life is about much more than setbacks and abuse.

6.

WHEN THE BOMB GOES OFF

Y ou, come up here. Yes, you!"

I couldn't believe it. That late summer Sunday, the whole family had gone to church together because an announcement had been made that a well-known prophet would be appearing that day to give out blessings and pray for solutions to our problems. And suddenly, this prophet was calling on Tía Rosie, who was sitting right there in the first pew.

"Step up here. I can see the anguish in your soul. Sexual abuse haunts you. Let us pray."

You could cut the silence with a knife. Rosie stepped forward and the prophet took her by the arm. He led her up to the pulpit and there—in front of my mother, my grandparents and nearly all my aunts and uncles and their own extended families—he asked us before God to intervene on behalf of her troubled soul.

My aunt didn't say a word. She was frozen stiff from the shock. Taking advantage of the confusion, I managed to slip away without anyone noticing me and went to hide in the bathroom.

It had been two years since we pinky swore never to tell our

secret. My father had stopped molesting me, and I was finally starting to feel like a normal girl again with no need to fear Fridays.
Rosie was sixteen by then and had a boyfriend of her own. And
now this! Oh my God!

I went into one of the stalls and knelt down to pray: *Oh my
Lord,* por favor, *don't let anyone notice that I'm gone, and don't let
my aunt say a thing, not a single thing, I beg you, dear God.* Then
I stopped to listen to the voices coming from the sanctuary, trying
to hear whether the prophet had finished his prayer. I was absolutely terrified of going out there and looking him in the eye. What
if he read my mind? What if he called me out as well? My hands
were shaking. All of a sudden, I heard the songs. *Uff, it's over,* I
thought. Relieved, I snuck back out and worked my way into the
crowd of people heading for the exit.

Much to my surprise, the whole Rivera family was out there in
the parking lot, acting as if nothing had happened. Nobody was
embracing Tía Rosie, nobody was asking for any explanations. My
own mother hadn't even opened her mouth, and she was always the
one to take the bull by the horns when it came to all family matters.

Rosie was silent. Everyone else was saying good-bye as usual.

"Okay, Juan, I'll see you at home, then," said my mother.

"Don't forget to call Gus later," my grandma reminded Tío
Lupe.

Kisses all around, and everyone got into their cars.

I didn't understand. I shot a glance at Tía Rosie for a second,
but she pretended not to see me.

Okay, I thought. *False alarm. Nobody believed it. The secret
is still safe.* Silly me. The secret was safe for a mere fifteen days,
which is the time it took for my mother to figure out how to tell
Rosie. Everyone else was frozen with the fear that the prophet's suspicions were true, and too afraid to ask Rosie about it face-to-face.

Everyone, that is, except for my mother, who was just waiting for the right moment.

It was Wednesday, September 23, 1997, to be exact. How could I ever forget a day like that?

We were with our cousins in the library doing homework. I had just started seventh grade, and my mom was very pregnant with Jenicka, the first of my two siblings who would come from her relationship with her second husband, Juan López.

My mother was at work doing the accounting at my grandfather's business, and she couldn't come pick us up until much later in the day. But, to our surprise, the one who showed up first was my tío Juan's wife, Tía Brenda.

"Come on, come on, we gotta go," she told us in a rush. We all piled into the car and instantly I knew it: *It's over. They finally found out*. The look on my aunt's face told me everything I needed to know. I couldn't have been more nervous.

We drove to the KIMOS offices on Market Street, which is where Tío Pete produced CDs of my grandfather's artists. Even back then, the whole family was involved in the world of music in one way or another. Those who didn't sing went into production or sales.

My mother was waiting for us there, sitting behind a desk in one of the tiny rooms. With her hair dyed red and freshly cut in a stylish bob, combined with her late-stage pregnancy, she looked very mature, though she was only twenty-eight. From the look in her eyes, I could tell that she'd been crying.

Sitting next to her was my tía Ramona, Tío Pete's wife, squeezing her hands nervously.

"Shut the door," my mother said as Brenda disappeared with my siblings. "Do you have something to tell me?"

I couldn't answer. All I could do was burst into tears. The pain I'd kept bottled up for so many years finally came bawling out.

"I'm sorry, I'm sorry, *mi princesa* . . . I'm so sorry!" Her tears seemed to overrun even my own. "Tell me Juan didn't do anything to you. Tell me that much, at least . . ." she implored, inconsolable.

Juan, my stepfather, was also there, standing by the door. His eyes were flashing with both grief and indignation, clearly upset that my mother would doubt him.

"No, Momma. Never. Just Dad. It was always just Dad. I swear . . ."

Juan, the poor guy. He was never anything but respectful toward me!

"Rosie just finished giving her statement. Now it's your turn, *mija*," my mother said, using her hands to smudge away the mascara running down her cheeks.

Two uniformed Long Beach police officers were waiting for me in the next office down the hall. Rosie had just emerged, leaving the door open behind her. She simply looked at me with fear on her face.

I went in and sat down. I wasn't afraid of the two men in uniform. The worst part—the thing I had feared most in my life—had already been done: confessing everything to my mother. Now all I had to do was to tell these men what they wanted to know. My mother was by my side, and she loved me. *Momma already knows and I can just be a kid again*, I thought to myself. That was all I could think about: the feeling of relief, even while giving the most gruesome details about the constant abuse.

I told them everything. Absolutely everything. Well, everything I could remember on that particular day. The officers were friendly, but didn't express much in the way of emotions. That was their daily bread there on the streets of Long Beach: listening to horror stories from families fighting for survival in a new country, lost amid the discrimination, the poverty, the harassment, the gangs—my beloved city. Every now and then they would stop me and ask, *Is everything okay? Are you doing alright?* Of course I was okay! I was great! My mom believed me right from the start, and that filled me with a strange sense of calmness. I was no longer alone with the monster that I'd locked away for so long in my heart, well hidden by the shame and fear of being called a liar or worse.

When I finished with the officers, I spent a moment with Tía Rosie there in the office hallway. Her eyes, like mine, were red and exhausted.

"I'm sorry, I'm just so sorry. I feel horrible. Your mother confronted me, and I couldn't lie. Please forgive me. I don't want you to have to live without your dad, but I just couldn't lie anymore!"

She was so nervous that I could barely understand her words.

We embraced. There was no need to say anything else. The secret we'd carried for so many years and that was eating at us from the inside was now out, and nobody doubted us. That would give us tremendous strength, which we would need when it came time to face what was still in front of us.

The next few weeks were like a long, strange nightmare. Detectives from the LBPD asked us to pretend that nothing had happened, that we keep going to school and work and that we tell no one. We didn't want to flush the quarry before the hunt: my father couldn't suspect that he was under investigation. The case was a complicated one, and they needed to collect more evidence before arresting him.

If my mother hadn't been pregnant at the time, we wouldn't have waited for an investigation to be conducted and an arrest warrant to be issued. She would have gone and killed him herself. I'm pretty sure she never even would have called the police. She'd have gotten a gun, gotten in the car and shot him dead.

And our dear, beautiful Jenicka managed to avoid a double

disaster: during the fifteen days of silence that followed, my mother—and her massive, pregnant belly—were going absolutely crazy.

One night I heard noises there in the house in Compton where we were living with my stepfather, Juan. I jumped out of bed and when I turned on the living room lights I was stunned by what I saw: my mother sitting there on the green leather couch, her face as hard as stone and her eyes fixated on the front door. She hadn't even noticed me yet, and between her legs she was holding a massive kitchen knife. My blood ran cold! Quietly I crept off to wake up Juan.

He embraced her and took the knife from her hands. The two of them cried in silence.

"I'm afraid he found out, and now he's going to come after us," my mother said. "If he walks through that door, I'll kill him. I swear to you, I'll kill him."

She spoke in a very measured tone of voice, and I don't have the slightest bit of doubt that she would have killed him. This was one of my biggest fears, and one of the reasons I was silent for so long: the fear of losing them both, one to murder and the other to jail.

∞

Halloween was approaching. My father was growing more impatient and starting to ask about why we hadn't visited him for a month. My mother, on the other hand, was coming up with a thousand excuses for not letting us go to his house.

And while we were anxiously waiting for the police to make a move, Jenicka arrived. The little one made her arrival two weeks early thanks to all the stress, but her presence gave us a breath of life and eased our pain.

"She's here! Our baby girl is here!" my grandma cried excitedly when I came home from school that day.

Back at the hospital, my mother lay in her bed, crying and laughing with Jenicka in her arms. She never let her baby out of her sight, day or night, always keeping her clutched to her chest.

On the great evening of Halloween, my mother was back at home with the most beautiful little baby girl in the world. And my father was on the phone, running his mouth about how much he wanted to take us trick-or-treating. We couldn't keep hiding like this. It just wasn't possible! The police were taking too long to act.

"Trick-or-treating? Are you serious?" my mother shouted into the phone. "You know what? I know what you did to my sister and my daughter, you son of a bitch! You'll be rotting away in jail!"

"You'll never prove it!" he retorted. The poor fool, he didn't even deny it. He just went straight to playing defense, like all people do when they're caught red-handed.

"I have them, you bastard! I have them!" she screamed, and then she hung up and immediately called the police. There was no time to lose! But nobody came to our aid.

On Halloween night, it's impossible to get a police officer on the phone. They're all out responding to emergencies or dressed up as Batman or Dracula enjoying the night with their families. Nobody was staked out, keeping a watch on my father during those crucial hours.

The next morning, the police paid a trick-or-treat visit of their own to his house. They knocked on his door, but here was the trick: the guy had packed up his clothes and ran. In a matter of hours, he and his girlfriend had up and disappeared, and their relatives all swore they didn't know anything about it. Everyone was as silent as a tomb.

A few months later, when my brother Tongo had just turned

eight, he confessed to us that he was ashamed of his father and everything about him. We could see the hatred in his eyes. He told us that the name Trinidad was no longer worthy of him, and that he had decided to change it. First he chose Max, like our dog, but then he settled on Michael, after Michelangelo, of the Teenage Mutant Ninja Turtles. All of his legal documents still show his name as Trinidad Marín, but ever since 1997, he's just been Mikey to us. Mikey Rivera.

I decided to stay with Marín. I was never ashamed of that last name, and I never stopped loving my father, no matter how sick people may think I am. My mother begged and begged me:

"My *princesita*, you're a Rivera. At least give me that joy. You're Janney Rivera," she would say.

"Momma, it's all I have left of him: the memories, both good and bad, and the last name," I'd always say, convinced that I'd never see him again.

Or so I thought.

7.

NO *QUINCEAÑERA*, NO SWEET SIXTEEN

Life after the scandal didn't stop there in the house in Compton where we were living. It was the first property that my mother ever bought with her own hard-earned money.

Despite all the pain and sorrow we were left with in the wake of the atrocities committed by my father, my mother kept on pedaling the bicycle of life, just as she always had. The problem was that I was just beginning my bitchy phase—adolescence—when I was acting more rebelliously and spending more and more time on the streets. Meanwhile, for the first time, my mother was really starting to dream about being Jenni Rivera, the big shot, the singer. This wasn't going to make things easy on either of us.

And poor Juan was caught in the middle of the storm. I remember not liking him at first. I was barely eleven years old when I met him, and still suffering my father's abuse in secret. Having another man around made me very nervous. On top of that, I was dying of jealousy at the idea of having to share my mother with another person. As if there weren't already enough people in that house!

The first day that Juan showed up with some of his belongings and started moving them into my mother's room, I searched through the dresser drawers and ripped a few pictures. Talk about a welcoming. And, of course, I got it good. My mother, strict as she was, gave me a serious whooping and sent me to bed. The look on my face was more than enough for him to know that I was the one who had given him such a warm welcome.

Much to my surprise, Juan didn't get angry. He just picked up the picture pieces and gave me a mischievous, knowing look.

And just like that—by always being cheerful and always having the time and patience to listen to us—he quickly won the hearts of my siblings and me. My new stepfather was very permissive with us and soon became our accomplice in nearly everything. For example, when my mother would put me on one of those super-strict, depraved diets, he'd secretly get me brownies and leave them for me under my pillow. Sneaky Juan! Maybe he wasn't the best husband in the world, but my God he was loved, and he didn't have an ounce of malice in that long, skinny body of his. He respected me so much and understood me so well that when my father ran off, I started calling him Dad. He deserved it. It's a title you have to earn; it's not handed out to just anyone who scores and gets his girlfriend pregnant. Being a parent is much more serious and much more important.

My mother started being more strict with me around that time, but honestly, she always had been. That's how the Riveras are with their children: never afraid to punish them or exact discipline, and you'd get whacked on the backside with a flip-flop before you could count to three. Sometimes I think it's because I was a bit of a spoiled brat and would answer back to everything, sometimes because of what had happened with my father. After she learned about my abuse, my momma started treating me more harshly. At first I didn't understand this, but as time went by I realized that she didn't want to spoil me or pamper me because of what had happened; she didn't want to treat me as if I were weak or a victim. That was one of her biggest fears. If anyone were to say, *Awww, poor Chiquis, look what happened to her!* it would seriously piss her off. Sometimes I think I was also a constant reminder of our family's greatest shame—the feeling of everyone having failed me—and she didn't quite know how to deal with those feelings. It must have been an incredibly difficult time for her, and I understand that it also must have been hard for her to deal with both me and with the past.

The fact of the matter is that whenever there was a problem, Juan would be the one to stick up for me and save my behind. He was a good father, but an unfaithful husband who turned out to be a bit of a womanizer and ended up putting my mother through a tough stretch of life.

But before he became a ladies' man and the fighting began, the daily relationship between Juan and my mother was an easy one. My momma could spend more time with us while Juan was working at a nearby factory. Back then, the kitchen in our Compton house made the place smell like a real home. Jenni the businesswoman was now cooking, taking care of us and looking after us. Juan was born and raised in the Mexican state of Nayarit, and like his fellow Mexican people, he was a huge baseball fan, and on the weekends he'd take us to play in all the neighborhood league games. My mother really enjoyed watching us play, and she had a great swing of her own as well. Baseball had always been another one of her passions.

In fact, Juan and Jenni shared many hobbies. Beyond the love they felt for one another, I saw them as two great friends. They laughed often, and liked to watch movies cuddled up in our huge green couch that took up the majority of the living room. Those were the days where I felt like I was a part of a normal family, which was something I never had before. But as was the case with everything else in our lives, those calm days only lasted for a short while.

That home sweet home suddenly came to an end thanks to the divine invention of caller ID and modern phones. My mother called an unknown number she found, and caught Juan on one of his adventures with a coworker. She kicked him out of the house in true Jenni style—revenge included—taking his clothes and starting a bonfire right there in the yard. Some time later, though, she forgave him, and Juan would be a part of our lives for a few more years, during which time he would give us another little brother and help push my mom to succeed. At this point she was working her way up the music industry ladder and discovering how much of a man's world it was. Neither of us really knew how to deal with it. And I wasn't aware of it at the time, but my mother was also going through so much.

∞

The Compton house was also the stage for the first big Jenni vs. Chiquis bouts. The living room with the huge green sofa became our ring. I was growing more and more unbearable by the day, and my mother's patience was wearing thin. Our relationship wasn't the same as it had been before the scandal.

I was in my freshman year of high school by then, and my grades weren't all that great. Straight Cs. And to my super-studious mother, Cs were akin to failure. When she was my age, she never got anything below an A.

"I was always the smart one in the family," she'd snarl at me when she saw my report cards. "Why does my brother Gustavo have all the sharp kids while I get the dumb ones?" I know that was her way to try to motivate me, but it still hurt and I wouldn't even dare to answer a question like that.

My first language, ever since I was a little girl, had been Spanish. Classes taught in English were hard for me, and I had trouble focusing on anything. I had so much responsibility. I had to clean and feed the kids before even starting my homework. And after everyone learned the secret about my father—that is, my own secret—I felt that the world owed me something, and that I deserved to be left alone.

And to top it all off, aside from being a great student, my mother was more of a nerd than a party girl and never had much of a social life, so when her first little boyfriend ended up getting her pregnant, whatever party there might have been was over before it started. But I was popular. I had a lot of friends, and it didn't take much for us to decide to skip class and go hang out. I was into the boys (though from afar, for obvious reasons). I liked dark lip liner and huge earrings. Like I was a little *chola* gangster! My mother would get frustrated and yell, "Who do you think you are? Take that off, don't be ridiculous!" It's hard to believe, but the woman who would go on to sing "*Las Malandrinas*" and really let her hair down had never been the sort of girl to hang out on the streets. Instead, she was a well-behaved daughter and a demanding mother. It was the men in her life—combined with the tough world of the artistic career she was just getting started on—that gradually turned her into the edgy, risqué Jenni. Later, we would see her become known as "La Diva de la Banda" and finally, simply, as "La Gran Señora." The thousand metamorphoses of the butterfly from the *barrio* were perfectly captured by her songs, and I happened to have first row seats to the show, and lived it with her each and every minute.

"Why are you being so hard on me?" I demanded tearfully. But what I didn't understand at the time was that my mother was just twenty-nine years old and already had four kids. She was still very young and having trouble dealing with everything that life had thrown on her plate.

"You didn't come into this world with a damn instruction manual, Chiquis! How the hell am I supposed to understand you?" she would yell when she just couldn't take it anymore, holding back tears of her own. "I never acted like that, so I don't know why you do."

There were so many things that we didn't understand about each other. Like the first time she kicked me out of the house, for example. I was fourteen, and right in the middle of finals during my freshman year at Jordan High School in Long Beach. During finals week, school was only half a day long, but instead of calling my mother, I went across the street to have a burger with some friends. After that, I went to the gas station where my stepfather would pick me up, always right at two thirty.

As soon as I got in the car, Juan handed me the phone.

"Chiquis, when you get home, don't you move. Just wait until I get there. You're in deep shit." It was my mother on the end of the line, cold and demanding.

"But, Momma!" I tried to explain.

"I don't want to hear it!" she screamed into the phone, ignoring my protest, and hung up.

"Your mom saw the other students heading home early and called the school. She knows you left at noon today," Juan informed me on the drive home.

When we arrived, Juan went straight to the garage to work on his cars and hide out from the coming storm. I didn't know what to do, so I pretended to fall asleep on the couch to avoid facing her when she returned home.

Bam! Slam! And then her very calm voice:

"You want me to whoop your ass, or do you want a different punishment?"

I didn't answer. I was terrified. My mother wasn't one to beat around the bush. She was as sweet and loving as she was strict and drastic. Filled with the anger that often characterized her, she grabbed a pair of massive scissors in one hand and a lock of my hair in the other, and then . . . snip, snip, snip! My hair began to fall by the fistful. And so did my tears.

Needless to say, at fourteen years old, my hair was my life! It was my personality, my pride and joy, what distinguished me from the other girls in my class. A magnificent mane, shining, coffee-colored, with soft and silky waves. My hair! The longest strand I had left among the patchy and raggedy hatchet job was *two inches*! I looked like I had mange.

"Now put on some shoes and get out of my house, bitch," she said, leaving the scissors on the table as she turned and walked away. That was the ruthless Judge Jenni. I decided I'd better just shut up and leave.

I laced up my sneakers, threw up the hood of my jacket to cover my shame and bolted out of there. It was around five or six in the evening.

Juan was still in the garage with the door open.

"Show your father what I just did to you!" my mother shouted from the front door,

I stood there in the front yard and pulled off my hood. And poor Juan started to cry. He really did love me, and it hurt him to see me like that. I think he also dreaded the cold-bloodedness that my mother could display from time to time.

I saw my mother's face growing angrier at the sight of Juan crying, and I just took off. I didn't want to get my stepfather in any more trouble. As I was running away down the sidewalk, I heard the fight starting.

"Are you crazy? Why would you do such a thing?" Juan demanded.

"Because I'm not to be fucked with."

Poor Juan. It was already too late. He was about to catch hell himself for having stuck up for me.

A few blocks down, I stopped at a pay phone and called one of my girlfriends from school. She told me I could crash at her place for a couple of weeks, at least until exams were through.

Two days later, a few other friends told me that my grandma was going from door to door like a crazy woman trying to find me, and that she was sick with worry. I called her and she begged me to come home to her house. And that's where I spent the entire summer of 2000. That's how I found myself back in my true home: the one that smelled of beans and Pine-Sol. I couldn't have ended up in a better place. A week after I arrived there, I turned fifteen years old.

For Latinas all over the world, your fifteenth birthday—your *quinceañera*—is the most important day of your life, after your wedding day. You can't have one without a big party, a mariachi band and a limo ride—unless, of course, you're celebrating in the kitchen with your grandma Rosa, who bought a small cake, and your tía Rosie, who loaned me some of her clothes. After dinner, I stared at the green phone hanging on the wall until well after midnight. It never rang.

Happy birthday, mija! I imagined my mother's voice in my head. But that phone didn't ring for me for two long months. It was the first time that my beloved mother had gone that long without speaking to me. The second would be many years later, but that occasion would have a very unexpected ending.

Feliz fifteen, I said to myself as I turned out the light and lay down to dream about long dresses, boys asking me to dance and all my friends dying of envy. It was then that I remembered that my mother never had a *quinceañera* party either. Back then, my grandfather was barely earning enough to feed six kids and keep a roof over their heads. Still, Grandpa Pedro—with all the love in the world—found a way to take her out to dinner and to drive her there in a convertible. Aaaah! Further proof that we never had any luck with this Mexican tradition. Not at all.

∞

Seven days later, it would be my mother's birthday. Mine is on June 26, hers is July 2 and Tía Rosie's is one day later, on the third. Normally, it was a week full of *fiestas* for the Riveras. But not that time.

Early that morning, I sent a fax to her office that read, *Happy Birthday Momma, te quiero mucho.*

Damn machines. Total silence. Years later, it would be Twitter that would fall silent during our fights.

Meanwhile, the slow summer days dragged on with nothing to do at my grandparents' house. I gained a ton of weight! I was feeling so depressed about losing my beautiful hair, my mother and my siblings that I started gorging myself there, in the kitchen that was always supplied with handmade tortillas.

My tío Lupe, who had started his singing career as Lupillo Rivera but had yet to earn enough to buy a new car, saw me as depressed as I was and said, "C'mon! Get in the car . . . I'm tired of seeing that stupid look on your face."

Lupe took me to a salon run by a few black women and paid $1,200 out of his own pocket to have them weave some braids into what was left of my hair. I picked the brown and blond ones, because I wanted to look like the singer Brandy. I sat on that hairdresser's chair for two whole days, from sunup to sundown. What a way to suffer, my God! But I managed to endure the torture without a complaint. I was so grateful to my tío Lupe for the beautiful gift, because I never would have started tenth grade with that awful, short hair.

Then, one morning, as I was fixing up my new Brandy-style look, my mother showed up at my grandma's house as if nothing had happened. She walked up to me, grabbed me by my muffin top bulging out over the top of my jeans and said, "Grab your things. It's time to come home."

I didn't ask, and I didn't protest either.

Once we got in the car, she didn't say, *Sorry, I love you*, or anything like that. We both sat there in silence, watching the other cars go by.

That's how we reconciled. With the muffin top!

"As soon as we get home, I'm getting rid of that ridiculous mop of hair, I'm putting you on the Zone Diet, and that's that," she warned me sternly.

"Okay Momma," I replied, trying to hide my immense joy. I knew I had finally regained my beloved mother. I didn't even care that she was about to start torturing me with her demands, her proteins and her carbohydrates.

Three days later, I started school with my short hair that she brushed up for me. Everyone was whistling at me during class, and I managed to lose the muffin top in a matter of weeks. That was the skinniest I've ever been in my entire life!

Jenni the Personal Trainer would even regulate the amount of water I could drink, and would make me dance in the garage for thirty minutes every day wrapped up in a trash bag. Wow. Happy Fifteenth, Chiquis!

Life went back to normal at our house in Compton. I went from fifteen to sixteen, and fell in love with a guy named José. At home, I was forbidden to have a boyfriend, and—though I liked boys and was a total flirt—I didn't dare go out with any of them. My secret still terrified me. What if someone tried to kiss me and found out what had happened? My life would be over!

José managed to overcome my fear. He was a rebel without a cause. Funny. Sympathetic. He dazzled me with his style and his personality. He got me to skip school. He was passionate about the famous street races in Compton.

And that's how I spent my sweet sixteen: watching the street races from the sidewalk, my sweaty hand gripping José's amid the deafening roar of the engines. The tricked-out cars burning rubber while the bets were placed, and the music of Notorious B.I.G. bumping in the background: "You know very well who you are . . . Don't let 'em hold you down, reach for the stars . . ." And then we all scattered at the sound of police sirens. Nobody wanted to spend the night in jail. We were the coolest kids in Long Beach, if only for a few hours.

However, when I was with José I always feared that he would find out what happened with my father. That fear was ever present in my life. Whenever we were together, he would try to kiss me; I was scared, but at the same time I liked it. I just let him hold my hand. I agonized, thinking I was dirty and used. *What if he finds out?* I thought to myself every time he tried to get to first base. Poor José. I think he could sense my fear, and after I stopped him a few times, he never tried again. Of course, after failing to hit a home run with me, he lost interest and soon enough left me for another girl. That's the game you play at that age. But I am forever grateful to him for those nights at the street races, when for a few hours my fears were silenced by the revving of engines on those industrial streets.

8.

I AM THE AIR FORCE

For years, before my mother and I started having our disagreements, I was her biggest fan. "Who's that?" asked one of the boys in my class, pointing to a picture I had on the front of my binder.

"My momma. She's gonna be as famous as Selena one day," I replied, with all the confidence in the world.

In the picture, my mom was posing in tight jeans and a sexy fuchsia top.

"Yeah, right!" he joked. "The great Jenni Rivera. Ha! That'll be the day!"

"Dumbass!" I yelled, and shoved him hard. I grabbed my books and walked away with my head held high, my ponytail swinging from side to side.

I had just started sixth grade, and we were living in the house on South Keene Avenue in Compton that my mother had worked so hard to buy when she was on her own. And, for the first time, my momma had talked with grandpa about recording some of the songs she had been writing herself, somewhat in secret. I was her number one fan. Dreaming together was fun, even if the rest of the world was mocking that poor single mom with all those kids.

One night, watching the Grammys on TV, Momma said, "What if I get serious about trying to sing?"

"*¡Sí, sí, sí!*" Jacqie and I encouraged her.

"You're gonna win a Grammy, Momma!" Mikey chimed in, excitedly.

Back then, Tío Lupe was just getting to be known and our reality was a very different one from the days of glamour and fame that were to come.

At school, I got made fun of because I wore hand-me-downs from my mother that were worn-out and didn't fit. At home we had tortillas with salt and beans for lunch and cereal for dinner. A poor man's menu, though we—in our innocence—didn't even notice it. Things got so bad that once, for a few months, my mother, the fighter, had to apply for benefits from the WIC program for women, infants and children. That was our reality. The odd jobs at the office weren't enough, and real estate sales had fallen off after the housing bubble burst in the mid-nineties.

I think the first time I realized that we were officially poor was Christmas of 1996. When I got home from school one day that December, I could see some lights through the window of the house. I ran inside to discover that the tree that my mother had lovingly placed next to the TV was no more than two feet tall, and that you could count the number of ornaments on one hand.

Yikes . . . there's not even enough space under that shrub to put a single present, I thought sadly.

I think that Christmas—with the beans, the cereal and that scrawny little tree—was the point when my mother decided that getting onstage would be the only way to turn things around. And why not? My tío Lupe was a performer, and he wasn't doing too badly for himself. Even my tío Juan was recording his own songs. My momma was just as much of a Rivera as they were, and music was the milk they were raised on.

Without waiting any longer, my mother got down to work and recorded "*Las Malandrinas*," though the song wouldn't become a hit until some years later. She spent the next few months performing here and there, but suddenly—and to everyone's surprise—she retired. Not even Juan, who had been working with her and attending all her local performances, understood what was going on.

"What got into you? Come on, Jenni, you're good!" he'd say.

"Son of a bitch! This is just too hard. It's a man's world out there. I just don't like it," she replied. We were all astonished, but that's all she told us, and we believed her.

∞

It wasn't until many years later, when I read her posthumous memoirs, that I found out the real reason why she hung up her microphone and almost walked away from music forever.

On one fateful night in 1997, while Juan was spending a few nights in jail for some trouble he'd gotten into, my mother was raped by a group of strangers after leaving a nightclub. This was just a matter of months before she discovered that Tía Rosie and I had been abused by my father. To this date, it pains me to write these words. Raped the same year she learned that her ex-husband, Trino, had raped her daughter and her sister. Just thinking about that leaves me short of breath.

How did we miss it? Tía Rosie and I were so frightened by our own situation that we didn't notice anything strange going on. We were all in survival mode. Plus, my mother did her best to keep it wrapped in the utmost secrecy for the rest of her life.

Now I have a better understanding of the horror I saw on her face that night when she was sitting in the middle of a darkened room with a knife in her hand, waiting for my father to be arrested. Hatred and fear had been mixed and stirred together into her own private hell.

Even in the midst of all that, my unwavering mother still gave birth to our beautiful little Jenicka, and she went back to her secretarial work and selling houses without objection. Decent, hardworking, loving and unwilling to complain or give in.

With these words, I hereby apologize to my mother, because we all failed her that year. We couldn't even begin to understand a fraction of the pain behind the tears she was shedding on that damn green sofa.

Time passed, and I—still oblivious to her secret—kept insisting: "But, Momma, singing is your calling. Let's go, let's go!"

We all begged and pleaded with her so much that finally—when her soul was more at rest—Jenni Rivera went looking for her scandalous "Malandrinas." She found the song, which she had first recorded before all the misfortune, and with the help of Juan, her unconditional fan, she started shopping it around to any radio station or nightclub who might be willing to play it.

"Hey, you're Lupillo Rivera's sister!" they'd say. Tío Lupe already had a big hit with his song "El Moreno" and his album *Puros Corridos Macizos*. I loved hearing them mention my uncle. My mother did too, at first, but later she grew tired of it. Who would ever take her seriously in the all-male world of *corrido* and *banda* music if she was just this guy's sister? We would! Us, her children. We took her very seriously.

So I'd go out on the weekends with my Jenni shirt and jean shorts to sell her posters and T-shirts at various fairs and festivals. My mother would carry little Jenicka around on her hip, and I'd lug

57

the diaper bag, CDs and boxes, while Jacqie and Mikey handled the snacks. We were an unbeatable team!

During those last two years of high school, it became clear to me that I was born to help out my mother. I felt—and I still feel to this day—that my job was to make the dreams of my family into a reality. Because, after all, despite all the difficulty we had to face, all the arguments and tragedies, her dream was our dream. She managed—and I say this very humbly—to accomplish what she did not only because she was a great artist, but also because I stayed at home taking care of her baby chicks. My baby chicks.

There's not always a great man standing behind every great woman. In this story, it was a daughter along with a whole family of parents, children and siblings who were ready to pitch in and help out.

By the time I'd turned seventeen, I was once again my mother's biggest fan and her most loyal support system. I focused my time on being at home with the kids. Juan left his own job so he could accompany my mother to her shows and help manage her tours.

I'd run home from school in the afternoons to fix supper, and I'd be blasting the radio there in the kitchen. And then one day . . . bam! They're playing *"Las Malandrinas"*! *Oh yeah!* I thought to myself as I folded the laundry, tossed out diapers and gave Jenicka a bath. *Now those fools back at school will see that I'm no liar. They're playing Jenni Rivera's song on the* Que Buena *radio station!*

As was always the case in my mother's life, as soon as the plane was about to take off, another baby showed up. But this time, our Johnny arrived with the proverbial loaf of bread under his arm. Finally!

The year 2001 had just kicked off and my tío Lupe was topping the charts with songs like "Despreciado" and "Gabino Barrera."

Wherever we went, people would shout, "Hey, it's Lupillo's nieces!" But eventually things started to change, and people started to call us "Jenni's daughters."

Tío Lupe's success was really what motivated my mother this time around. She decided not to put her career on hold during her pregnancy. After she gave birth, she handed me that baby with a perfectly straight face and said to me, clear as day:

"*Mija*, I really need you. Now more than ever."

And with that, from day one, Johnny became my baby.

From Tucson to Bakersfield, from El Paso to Raleigh, my mother would call us at the house before she went onstage. It was her good-luck move. She couldn't perform without that phone call.

"How's my king?" she'd ask, a hint of sadness in her voice.

"Don't worry, Momma. Johnny's asleep in my arms. He's fine. Now go out and show them what you're made of. Knock 'em dead out there!"

"I love you, *mija*," she'd say. When we hung up the phone, I'd imagine the crowd applauding as Jenni Rivera walked confidently out onstage, her head held high, before bending at the waist, her long blond hair flowing forward in a dramatic bow.

For the next year, my mother worked hard, made sacrifices and performed at every town, ranch or club to which she was invited. Jenni Rivera never turned down a gig. All she saw was bread for her children. Or rather, steak! Because our menu was about to change.

One evening, when we were all lounging around the house, my mother burst in with enthusiasm: "What are you doing on the couch? Turn off the TV. Come on! Up! Get in the car! Let's go, let's go!" In the blink of an eye, she dragged us, grumbling, out of the house. "I want to show you something."

Without offering any more details along the way, she drove us to Corona, about forty miles from Compton, which had been our home for the past year, and forty miles from our beloved Long Beach.

"Look, this is your new home," she said as she parked the van at the base of a hill. At the top of it sat a two-story building surrounded by a huge field.

The looks on our faces when we walked in through the double doors!

"It's a freaking mansion!" I couldn't contain my shock. "Does this mean we're rich now? Oh, shit . . . !"

My mother started laughing and, with a mischievous wink, she said, "It means we're blessed. Very blessed."

In practical terms, it meant we had gone from eating tortillas with salt to a 7,000-square foot house in just a couple of years.

As the golden age Mexican film actress María Félix once said, "Money is important in life. It does not give you happiness, we all know, but it sure calms the nerves." That's God's honest truth. Our lives improved remarkably. Now my mother could provide her younger children with the things that I never had: bigger rooms, better doctors, better schools and better food in the fridge.

And there, in our new home in Corona, with me in my new role as mother, I celebrated my eighteenth birthday and my high school graduation.

People always assume eighteen is the age when you decide what you're going to do with your life. And even though I was happy helping out my mother, I still had dreams of my own. Secretly, like any other girl, ever since I was little, I'd close my eyes and picture myself either singing or acting. I wasn't sure which. At the time, it was just innocent fantasizing while searching for Mikey's other shoe under the couch or washing Jenicka's hair with No More Tangles baby shampoo.

"I've made my decision," I said to my mother one night after she came home, exhausted from yet another flight. "Mom, I'm joining the Air Force. I'm gonna shave my head, and the four years I'm serving will give me time to think about what I want to be in life."

My mother was incredulous. "I don't understand . . ."

"Yes, Momma. The Air Force will pay for college."

"I am the Air Force, *mija*. I break my back each and every day so that you can have what you want. You don't need anybody to pay for anything. You've got it all right here. I'm the one who needs you here, with the kids, Chiquis. I can't do it without you. I'll give you a job, I'll pay you cash!"

And without another word, I became—in addition to a mother to my siblings—my mother's personal secretary, wardrobe stylist, counselor, accountant, shopper and even the cheerleader of the new *Diva de la Banda*. And I have to admit that I liked it. Feeling so needed by my mother and my siblings was the best form of compensation. I couldn't imagine a better way to be paid for spending 14 to 20 hours a day without a break.

With all the hard work and the new house in Corona came *la vida loca*. Especially after the inevitable split between Juan and Jenni. The father of two of my siblings and my own great partner in crime just packed up his bags one day and moved into a small apartment not far away. My mother just couldn't take it any longer. This time, it had nothing to do with jealousy or infidelity. Instead, it was their constant arguments back and forth about work: "You did this," "I did that," "You don't do anything," "I left my other gig to do this with you." They just couldn't stand the pressure, and my mother exploded one day when she came home to find Juan relaxing comfortably on the couch, watching a baseball game with moisturizing cream all over his face. She, on the other hand, was exhausted, having just returned from the road, and she asked for a separation right then and there. The former *mejores amigos* could no longer stand one another. Thanks to their mutual stubbornness, they put an end to their eight-year relationship.

Juan begged me to help him out and talk some sense into my mother. He didn't want to lose her, and he didn't want a divorce. But I told him that it would be for the best if we all went our own ways. I loved Juan, but I just couldn't stand another shouting match in that splendid kitchen, surrounded by white marble and expensive appliances. The fact is that when couples argue, it's just as ugly in a Compton kitchen as it is in a beautiful mansion. And, at that point, separating was the only solution.

Of course, on that day when he came to pick up the last of his things, I got super sad. My siblings were losing their father, though not entirely, because he would still visit them often. And I was losing a close friend—someone who respected me and understood me, even during the most awful moments of my life.

Shortly after Juan left, things started to change in Corona. It all started with the clothes.

"Chiquis, I need you to buy me something more modern, more daring, *mija*," my mother asked me once before I made my regular weekly trip to Macy's.

I was in charge of filling her closet with dresses for her performances, and for buying the jewelry she'd wear onstage before taking it off and throwing it into the crowd for her fans. There were dozens of necklaces and bracelets flying through the air every month!

Seeing her starting to dress sexier didn't really bother me. In fact, I was flattered when my friends would say to me, *Wow, your mom looks hot!*

What concerned me was the attitude that came with the clothes. It seemed as if she was trying to regain her lost adolescence, trying to compete with God knows who about who looks younger. Her miniskirts, her secret little phone conversations and her constant partying with her friends were all driving me crazy!

But gradually I got used to the new Jenni. For the first time, we were starting to see each other as friends, not just as mother and daughter. She had stopped being so strict with me, and was now treating me more as an adult. For my part, I'd stopped criticizing her for her craziness, and had learned to accept the fact that Momma wasn't one to come home and put on a dress by Ann Taylor or capri khakis from the GAP.

The newly single Jenni had officially let her hair down. It was her first time being on her own, strong, with money in the bank and no man to order her around, since she was fifteen. Nothing was gonna stop her now!

One boring Thursday evening between shows following the release of her latest album, *Mi Vida Loca*, the new Jenni surprised me:

"Come on," she said.

"Where are we going?"

"To get a piercing. Didn't you say you always wanted one?"

"Yes, Momma, but not today! And with you?"

"With me, or never" was her devilish offer.

Thirty minutes later, we were both sitting in chairs at the first tattoo parlor we could find open at that hour of the night.

We both opted for a belly-button piercing. Mine healed perfectly, but my mother's got infected because she didn't take good enough care of it, and I forced her to remove it. The daughter scolding the mother. Those were crazy times, no doubt!

And it was during this new *vida loca*, each of us found love. Her first.

In the beginning, my mother hid the news from us, but since you can only keep these things under wraps for so long, she eventually invited him over for a barbecue so she could introduce him to us. And oh my God! I almost died. He was bald, he looked like a *cholo*—a gangster—and was barely older than me! If my math is right, I was eighteen when I met him, and he was no more than twenty-two, which made him eleven years younger than my mother.

But the funny thing is that I really dug him from the moment I met him. Ferny's like that. He's a good guy. Very funny. And he defended us and calmed my mother when she would yell at us.

With his *cholo* style and his young age, Ferny gradually earned everyone's affection. Jacqie and Mikey absolutely worshipped him, since Ferny could always make them laugh. And soon enough, I learned that this bald guy really knew how to get the best out of my mother's career. He came up with creative and rebellious new ideas, and talked to her about street fashions.

"You gotta bring out your inner thug," he'd say to Momma. "Act like the chick from Long Beach that you are."

And wow, did my mother ever start channeling her inner thug and her inner Long Beach! Ferny helped give her an edge, and *Vida Loca* was hitting the top of the radio charts. My mother would later confess to me that he impressed her in other ways too.

"This is the man who made me a real woman. I'm thirty-four, and this is the first time I really enjoyed sleeping with someone," she blurted out one night at a friend's party, after getting a few drinks in her.

"Oh no, Momma! I don't wanna hear about that!" I was laughing and dying from embarrassment at the same time.

My mother was going through a period of change in her life, and the fact of the matter is that I had to get used to my new friend Jenni. But at the same time, my mother never failed to punish me, advise me, protect me, take care of me or control me. We were friends, yes, but only for short periods of time, because Jenni had always been a great mother to me, right up until the very end.

And maybe it's because Jenni was too Jenni for Ferny, a kid from the streets of the San Fernando Valley, that their relationship became a bit of a tug-of-war, as had happened before. Ferny would disappear for days before coming back looking skinny and with a distant look in his eyes, as if he were a zombie. That, combined with my mother's character, which was never passive, and her career, which was becoming more successful by the day, resulted in explosive fights.

And as she always did with the men in her life, during one of those arguments, my mother said *no más* and kicked him out of her life. But not completely.

Ferny was relegated to the lover or friend with benefits who would step in between the future boyfriends, breakups and reconciliations. This guy from the streets of the Valley had worked his way so deeply into my mother's heart that she never stopped loving him. Fernando, her *pelón*.

Those were some eventful years, living in that house on the hill. Years that I remember fondly every time I drive down the 91 Freeway.

But it was also during our time in Corona that we received some other devastating news: the ghost of my father was not far away. It was so close, in fact, that we couldn't believe it—just off that same highway! This ghost who, after disappearing completely for all those years, was coming back into our lives to reopen old wounds and cause even more harm. It was inevitable.

9.

MORE KISSING THAN TIME IN BED

I met him at that house in Corona, while my mother was living her own great love story during those crazy years.

"Chiquis, you're in charge of calling everyone, scheduling the DJ and ordering plenty of beer," my mother said, laying out the instructions very clearly. "But I'd better not catch you flirting with any of his buddies!"

This, of course, was regarding the birthday party she wanted us to organize for her beloved Ferny.

It was 2004, and at eighteen, I was more celibate than a nun. Between my fears of the past, and taking care of the house, the kids and my mother's career, I just didn't have any time for going out with guys. And, needless to say, my momma protected me like a South Central pit bull. No guy was good enough for her! But I think it was just her fear of me getting hurt.

I spent that whole week getting ready for the barbecue on Saturday, and that's when Héctor appeared.

Héctor had been invited by one of Ferny's friends, but he

wasn't a direct friend of the *pelón*, so technically he was outside the scope of the limits my mother had set up.

Just like it happens in the movies: he looked at me, I looked at him and bam! Love at first sight.

"Can I help you with the cake?" he offered quickly, and helped me set things up in the backyard.

Early on during the party, I didn't dare talk to him much. Plus, I was super busy attending to all the guests. Including the strippers that Héctor himself had invited!

The girls were starting to get really annoying, especially when they started asking me to let them into the house so they could get ready. They complained about being outside in the yard, and demanded that we move the whole party and all the guests inside so they could perform their dance in the living room.

They made their way inside and that made me snap. "Everyone outside! On the patio now!" And with that, they went back outside.

"Why'd you throw them out?" Héctor immediately protested.

"Because nobody's allowed inside. Party rules. Patio yes, house no," I said, fuming.

"But they're cold!"

"I don't care! That's their job, to get naked wherever they are!" I wasn't about to budge. Rules are rules, and those girls were acting like they were the shit.

Héctor looked at me like he wanted to shove me into the pool for running my mouth off, but he decided it would be better to go and try to calm down the strippers, who were now threatening to leave without performing.

In the end, they did their dance in the backyard, and went off to take their show elsewhere. Later on, after midnight, when the party was starting to die down, I felt bad about what had happened and went to apologize to Héctor.

"Can I get you a drink?" I asked him, peacefully this time.

"Okay, but only if you let me take a picture with you," he answered, all serious. "I just need some help finding the batteries to my camera. I think I left them in the car."

I think it was just a line to get me away from the crowd, because once we got to the car, he got right into it: "Give me your number," he asked, not wasting any time.

"Why don't you give me yours?" I countered.

"Here," he said, handing me one of his business cards.

"Oh, shit!" I exclaimed when I saw he worked for Estrella TV. "My mom's not gonna like this!"

"We'll see," Héctor said, crossing his arms like a totally flirtatious little *cholo*.

It was a month before I could admit to my mom that I was going out with Héctor.

When she found out, she said, "That dude just wants to date you because he works on TV and you're the daughter of someone famous. He's out to get something."

"No, Momma. I swear he's a good guy. Please, please, please," I begged.

"Okay. Invite him over for dinner on Friday. We'll double date: you with him and me with Ferny."

Hmmm. It wasn't like my mother to agree so easily. I knew her too well. Clearly she was up to something. My momma was an expert when it came to strategies and surprises.

That Friday, Héctor came over wearing a nice black sweater and carrying a six-pack of Michelob Ultra, my mother's favorite beer. He looked scared to death, but she made an effort to make him feel at home. She fixed steak and shrimp for everyone, but still I couldn't stop sweating throughout the entire meal, waiting for the bomb to drop.

Near the end of the evening, my mother fired the shot: "Look, son, if you want to be Chiquis's boyfriend, I don't see a problem with that. But you'll have to give up your television job first."

No sooner said than done! A few weeks later, Héctor left Estrella TV, and not only that, he started working with my mother on a couple of projects. He was very smart for a twenty-two-year-old: if you can't beat 'em, join 'em! That's how he got not only the daughter to like him, but the mother as well.

Héctor and I were truly in love. I was dying to get closer to him physically, and yet I was terrified. We spent months just making out.

Héctor was very patient, and he proved to me that not everybody who comes into your life is there to hurt you. He already knew something about my past; I think Ferny told him some of the rumors, but he didn't seem concerned about that. Much to the contrary, in fact. He said he understood, and that he was willing to wait until he'd earned my trust.

And he did.

It happened one night at his house. I worked up my courage and said to myself, *It's now or never.* I even asked if we could leave the lights on. I couldn't let the darkness of the past ruin such a beautiful moment.

It wasn't the sexiest chapter of my life, or even the most exciting, but still I cannot describe the feeling it gave me to have Héctor there, beside me, hugging me, even after we finished. In my mind, I thought that once he finished, he'd just get dressed and leave. That's how I thought sex worked: first I use you, and then I leave you. And why wouldn't it be like that, if that was how I'd been treated my entire life? It was with infinite tenderness that Héctor taught me that two people can actually respect each other and each other's bodies. But even with so much love, it still took me almost two full years until I learned to relax enough to be able to enjoy some intimacy. Bless my Héctor and his patience.

But that night, after returning home, my biggest fear was no longer the touch of my boyfriend's hand, it was whether or not my mother would find out! She could tell just by looking me in the eye. Jenni the FBI special agent. Luckily, nobody was awake at that hour and I could go straight to sleep.

Time went by, and while my momma must have been worried that I'd eat the cake before dessert and get knocked up, she never mentioned anything about it. That's how much she loved and respected Héctor. Her maternal instincts were telling her that her daughter was in good hands.

My romance with Héctor lasted for several years, including the typical breakups and separations that happened every once in a while. We were still so young at the time. At one point, he asked me to marry him, and I, being young and foolish, said yes, even though deep down I knew I wasn't ready. I felt somehow obligated, perhaps because of all the patience and understanding he'd given me. And in the end, we never even set a wedding date. All of our joint promises and plans were broken off when we both ran out of patience and love.

∞

During that time, my mother's career was demanding more and more of our time, and there came a point where I felt I had to choose between Héctor and my mother and siblings. There just wasn't enough time for everybody! Eventually, he couldn't wait any longer, and I didn't have the strength to continue on the way we were, and our separation was official.

"One day your mom's gonna give you a swift kick in the ass, and then you'll realize what you missed out on," Héctor said, very upset. And he was right, because that kick did come, and it hurt even more than he had predicted. Still, though, I don't regret the decisions I made. My mother and my family always have and always will come first and foremost.

And that's how I left the man who taught me to love fearlessly.

But there was one more love that I haven't talked about from those years we spent in the house in Corona. And this one was especially unique.

During one of my breakups with Héctor, early on in our relationship, we stopped talking for a number of months and I devoted myself to spending more time with my girlfriends. One of them was named Karla, and I used to go out with her a lot.

"What's up with Karla?" my mother asked, shooting from the hip as she always did, though still with great accuracy and without me ever seeing it coming.

"Nothing, Mom. She's just a friend. My best my friend right now," I replied, super nervous.

"I hope so, *mija*. I hope so."

Yikes. I swear that sometimes my mother had a sixth, or even a seventh, sense.

Karla (let's call her that to avoid bringing up any trouble from the past) and I met through my brother Mikey. She was two years younger than me, but infinitely more intelligent and intellectual than the rest of my friends. Even so, my mother never liked her from the day they met. She thought she was a smart-ass, a know-it-all and a bit tomboyish.

With or without my mother's blessing, we started texting one another. The texts gave way to long talks on the phone. We ended up talking for entire afternoons or nights.

I don't know at what point we realized that this friendship was turning into something deeper. We both felt confused by it all. She had never kissed a girl before, and neither had I. And then suddenly, we did. It was a beautiful, honest kiss that left us feeling scared and excited at the same time. After that, it was several days before we saw each other again. I swear, we were both so embarrassed.

But the need to keep talking to each other won out in the end, and we ended up together, spending hours and even days cuddling on the couch, watching movies and looking for a love that we didn't know where to find.

To be honest, during those early months of my relationship with Héctor, I had failed to satisfy him sexually, the way he'd hoped and deserved. That was the reason for our breakup at that time. I was still very traumatized and I felt that this new love with Karla didn't require the bed part, which I wasn't ready for.

We never got to the point where our platonic romance became something sexual. We never went past kisses, and we were so platonic, in fact, that we loved writing long letters to each other in which we'd confess the most beautiful feelings. I hid these letters in my room, buried under mountains of boxes and coats, but my mother, the Russian spy, didn't take long to uncover them during one of her secret operations in my closet. And we were screwed: with that, our relationship was over.

As usual, my mother had her strategy all planned out, and she waited until the perfect time to confront me, one evening when we were alone in the house.

"I'm going to ask you again, Chiquis, what's going on with Karla?" she asked, out of the blue, while putting on her makeup in her bedroom. "If you continue seeing her, I'll take away all the benefits you enjoy as my daughter. As long as you live under my roof, you'll respect my rules."

"Momma, it's not fair," I protested, because at this point it was useless to deny anything. "You have a lot of gay friends. Don't come at me with this now."

"I don't judge or condemn them, but in my house, I'm telling you no. I have a lot of lesbian friends and I love them all, but I have also seen how much they suffer, and I don't want that life for you. I don't want to see you cry." My mother finished putting on her lip gloss with an emphatic flourish and blew a kiss into the mirror. End of discussion.

The next day, I told Karla that we needed to end things. She was angry, she didn't understand and she told me to go to hell. I was heartbroken, but I knew my mother only too well. To keep seeing Karla would have started World War III. And after all, I wasn't even sure about my own feelings. It was better to leave this as what it was: a simple adventure.

Now Karla has a fantastic boyfriend, and even though we didn't end up being the best of friends, we both know that what happened to us back then happens to plenty of girls. It's a part of adolescence, part of beginning to uncover who you are. Neither of us regrets what happened or feels ashamed about it, and this episode is part of my history, and—of course—hers.

After Karla, I never again did I feel attracted to another woman. The mini-romance I had with her helped me to clarify the fact that I like men. It's true that it was a woman who made me "play house." It's true that I grew up with a lot of doubt. But that doubt had finally disappeared.

However, this episode never fully left my mother's mind, and it would—during our final days together—rouse suspicion and a strange sense of jealousy, along with our most brutal and final fight.

10.

HOW TO JUDGE A BROKEN HEART

The phone next to the bed rang very early that Saturday morning in April of 2006.

I was in Vegas, which is where I always seem to be when the most intense, shocking news breaks.

"*Mija*," said the voice on the other end of the line. It was my mother, and she sounded serious. "I just want you to know that they arrested your father."

Héctor saw the look on my face when I hung up. At this time Hector and I hadn't yet broken off our engagement. Immediately he hugged me. He could tell that another great wave of torment was heading for my family and me. I was nearly twenty-one years old, and I was about to resurrect something that I'd left buried away since I was twelve.

Later that same night, back home, my mother told me everything: about how he'd been seen several times in the past year, once driving down the 405, and how my tío Lupe chased after him, but he managed to get away. The next time, it was my tía Rosie. She ran into him at a NORMS in Lakewood. Rosie was petrified with fear, and he ran out of the restaurant as soon as he saw her. Everyone knew that he was somewhere in the vicinity and that it was only a matter of time.

This encouraged my mother, who decided it was time to use her well-earned fame as La Diva de la Banda to close the outstanding account with the law. That year, my mother was enjoying success on an international level, with thousands of fans following her from here to Mexico. It wouldn't be hard to put her army on the alert.

After asking Rosie and me for permission (I agreed, but only very reluctantly), my mother revealed in a radio interview that her former partner, José Trinidad Marín, was a fugitive from the law and facing criminal charges for having abused us. She asked anyone who saw him to immediately turn him in to the authorities. The repercussions this had throughout the media were the size of the fear itself! Jenni Rivera's former husband was a *pedophile*!

A few days later, after another radio interview, a man called my mother to say: "I am an agent of the United States government, and I am at your service. We're going to find him. I promise you that."

Nobody had bothered to tell me that, with this call, the family had accepted the help of no more and no less than the FBI. They kept that totally secret from me.

This mysterious agent managed to track down some vital clues, and thanks to a tip from another fan, he was soon able to obtain an address.

Early that morning, Trino went out to water the yard at the address in question. He had no idea that he was already being watched. He was very well groomed, as usual, and they arrested him right then and there. He didn't put up much of a fuss when they slapped the handcuffs on him. The crazy thing is that he was living just three exits down from the road that led to our new home in Corona, right there in Riverside County. We were practically neighbors! And all this time, we thought he'd run off to another state or was in hiding out in Mexico!

He'd been there for two years, living and working under one of his brothers' names. Life had treated him well. He owned several apartments and had fathered a daughter with Dora, the same, faithful girlfriend we already knew.

"Now he'll pay for everything he did to us." Those were Mikey's words to me when he saw me arrive that night, back from Las Vegas.

"Why the hell didn't anyone tell me anything? What's with this family? Isn't he my father?" I yelled at everyone.

I was furious and felt deeply betrayed.

Jacqie was silent. She was very young when the abuse had taken place and she never stopped loving our father; or rather, she had never stopped needing him. Like me, she never dared to tell anyone that we still loved him in our own way. Clearly, we were the only two people who were not happy with the news about his arrest. Would people see us as some kind of monsters for thinking and feeling this way? Jacqie was the only one who understood me. We didn't even need to talk about it. An exchange of glances was enough for us to know how much this news hurt us. That's why love and hate are such strange emotions. They don't make any sense, much less in the heads of two young girls.

In Tía Rosie's mind, however, it was all very clear. Now was the time to demand justice. She had witnessed the arrest that morning herself, sitting in a van with dark, tinted windows alongside the FBI agent. She was scared to death, but she also felt sorrow for my father's youngest daughter, who was also there, sobbing inconsolably. After it all went down, the agent gave Rosie the handcuffs they'd used during the arrest and she decided to keep them. That bothered me. What a strange trophy! Why would she want to keep a memento of that dark day in her dresser drawer? The worst part about it is that she gave them to my mother a few months later, so that morbid souvenir ended up somewhere in my own house, who knows where.

By saving them, you're putting these handcuffs on your own soul, I thought, but I didn't dare criticize them. I, more than anyone else, knew how much Rosie had suffered. I had been the silent witness to the transformation of my aunt into a bitter, sad and reclusive teenager—all for the man who gave me life, and who would later destroy it for both of us.

The next day, when the arrest of Jenni Rivera's ex-husband broke all over the news, I became the most famous victim of sexual abuse at the time. My name and my face were everywhere, right next to my father's mug shot.

"Why did you do this to us?" I screamed at my mother while scanning the awful headlines on the Internet. "And don't tell me it was to stir up publicity for your career!"

"How dare you think that! All I want is justice. That asshole has to pay. I won't let him lay a finger on another girl ever again. It's about justice, *mija!*" she repeated one last time. Her eyes were ablaze like those of a fierce lioness, while mine were filled with the tears of a lost cub.

"But, Momma, do we really have to go through with all of this? I mean, it was over ten years ago. Dad already has another daughter who's gonna miss him just like we did. They could just let him go." Nobody seemed to understand that my heart was divided: he was the assailant, but he was also my father!

"No, Chiquis. At this point, it's out of my hands. There's no turning back now. It's the law."

Over the next few hours, as news of the scandal grew and the paparazzi began to surround our house, my grandma Rosa, with her love and prayers, made sure that I understood everything:

"Do not judge your mother. You must accept the righteousness of God. Do this for all three of you: for Jenni, for Rosie and for you too. In this, you are all suffering equally."

Okay, then. I accepted my fate. We would take this to court. My grandma was right about everything. In the midst of my own pain, I lost sight of the fact that I wasn't alone in this boat. God would take care of us and he would take care of my father as well.

Three days later, we were summoned for the arraignment at the city courthouse in Long Beach.

"Chiquis," Rosie whispered in my ear when we pulled into the parking lot. "I want him to publically ask us for forgiveness. You too, baby. The two of us deserve that much."

I gave her a hug, and we walked, hand in hand, up those cold stairs to the second floor. The circus would begin when the judge brought down his gavel.

My father came into the room wearing the orange jumpsuit that country prisoners wear. He was surrounded by guards, and they sat him near his family and friends. On the other side of the courtroom sat the Riveras, enraged, waiting like caged tigers.

I panicked when I looked him in the face. He looked good, serious and relaxed, sitting there in front of his wife and daughter. Suddenly, just like that, out of nowhere, I thought to myself, *Has he missed us? In all this time, has he missed us?*

The hearing that day lasted only an hour and ended relatively calmly after the nine criminal charges were read, which included statutory rape, aggravated assault and continued sexual abuse of a child. It was all more or less what the attorneys had told us to expect. My father didn't seem surprised by the long list of offenses; in fact, he looked emotionless, and he didn't turn to look at us even once, not even when he was being led, in handcuffs, out the door.

The trial itself began four months later, in the summer of 2006, and it would last for over ten months. During that time, I would become the most hated being on the planet when it came to my father's family, who looked at me with such disdain and disgust that I felt paralyzed. I swear, I couldn't even feel my legs every time I saw them.

The legal process also began to have an effect on the relationship between Rosie and me. Rather than uniting us, which is what I thought would happen, it began to drive us apart. Her thirst for justice was obsessive, whereas I couldn't bring myself to hate my father, no matter how much I tried, and no matter how much she tried to convince me. Also, that same year, my aunt had gotten deeply involved in my tío Pete's church, and had decided to give her heart over to Christ. *Why can't she take some of those lessons about mercy and pity and put them into practice?* I would ask myself.

Clearly, I had tried to put myself in her position, but she was making no efforts to walk a mile in the shoes of a confused, conflicted daughter. Oh well. The show must go on. The curtain has already been raised.

Next, the depositions began. Growing up, Rosie and I never shared even the tiniest detail about the abuse we had suffered at the hands of the same man; shame prevented us from doing so. And during the trial, we didn't listen to one another either. When she gave her testimony, I would be led out of the room. When it was my turn to take the stand, it was her turn to wait outside. That's what the law required. Rosie was called to testify first.

Am I sick? Did I just make all this up in my head? Maybe it never happened! After all, at the end of the day, Trino was a good dad! These thoughts were driving me crazy while I waited there, alone in the hallway, for my turn. I felt a thick fog enveloping my brain, keeping me from remembering anything. My mind went completely blank.

Half an hour later, they brought me back into the courtroom. I sat down next to Rosie. Now it was my father who was on the witness stand. And all of a sudden—when I heard his voice after all those years, and I heard him accuse me of being a liar—the clouds disappeared from my mind. He repeated the word three times: *Chiquis lies, lies, lies.* Half from sheer courage and half out of pure shock, all the memories flooded clearly back into my mind. Down to the last detail. His touch, his manipulations, his lies. Even those blue metal bunk beds that used to taunt me. And in the midst of all those images bombarding my mind, one in particular surprised me: I saw myself in the backyard at my grandparents' house on Gale Street. I pictured it so clearly that it gave me the chills. I couldn't have been more than three years old. I was wearing a pink dress. Of course I would have a dress like that! My father would sit me on his lap and caress me underneath that dress. I remembered just a few seconds of touching, and then he would let me go. How was it possible that I never remembered that happening before that very day, sitting in court? But, more importantly, it meant that the day after the beach was not the first time. There had been previous attempts, and who knows why he would let me go. Oh no, no way was I crazy. I wasn't making up anything. That dress confirmed it. It had all been real, and now they were going to hear me out.

Less than an hour later, I was taking the stand. I went up there with every intention of being brave, but the tears took over as soon as I sat down on that awful chair. I had to ask the judge for a few minutes to calm down. Once I composed myself, I looked first at the defense attorney before focusing on the crowd. Eventually, I worked up the courage to look at the faces of my family and then into the eyes of my father. He stared back with a cold look of infinite sadness. With silent lips, he slowly uttered the words *I love you* addressed directly to me.

Jacqie saw it as well, and we both began to cry. Yet again, this man was toying with our emotions, trying to manipulate us. And it hurt! Everything went blank again. Did he really still love me? Thousands of images raced through my mind, and I just wanted to take off running and get as far away from that horrible gray room as fast as possible.

First, his lawyer brought up the police report from 1997. Still mentally blocked up by the fear from that *I love you*, I couldn't remember what the hell I'd said back then. My answers were a disaster.

During one of the breaks in testimony, my mother grabbed both my hands, kissed them, and said: "*Mija*, your words are going to help so many little girls out there who are suffering just like you did. You can be their voice now. You can help them, through your story. Be strong, baby. I'm with you."

With her words still ringing in my ears, I returned to the witness stand, and bam! It all came back to me as if it were yesterday. I was answering even the most rigorous questions without hesitation. Not even the shame of testifying in front of my grandparents, my siblings and even Héctor, who was also there in the courtroom, could stop me. Sometimes I was forced to bring up details involving the penis or vagina, and other things that were so disgusting they made me blush. But I was not about to be intimidated. I was going to show the world that I was not a liar.

The only one I felt deeply embarrassed for was my tío Juan. I was his beloved little girl, and he was my hero, my father figure. If it hurt me to tell this story, imagine what it was like for him to hear it that day, in that room, staring into the face of my father, who denied each and every allegation with a shake of his head.

These court appearances felt endless. Entire days spent listening to lawyers, laws, criminal codes and the most disturbing evidence you could imagine, like the medical examination the police performed on Jacqie in 1997. According to the results of that examination, her abuse had started as early as two years old, though, of course, she wouldn't remember any of that. There were so many details that I had never wanted to hear!

In October, someone paid the half-million-dollar bail that had been set by the judge. In a weird coincidence, it was a member of my dad's family who bore the same name as my beloved tío, Juan Rivera.

That evening, my father walked into court on his own two feet, free, dressed in a suit and tie and accompanied by his family. He looked more composed, and even arrogant. He dared to look at us directly.

At the conclusion of that session, both families left at the same time through the same door, and everyone's temper was flaring. *How could they let him out of the joint, even after he paid bail?* The Rivera clan protested indignantly. And as you might have expected, the tigers started going at each other right then and there.

Mikey was the first to approach my father in the hallway; he threw a punch right at my father's head because, according to him, Trino gave my tío Lupe an arrogant look, and he just couldn't control himself. Suddenly everyone was biting, punching and kicking in all directions. It was war between the two families! And amidst all that fighting, my father kept that same arrogant little grin on his face, while my mother was screaming bloody murder: "You son of a bitch! You're gonna pay for everything you did, you bastard!"

Thank God my tío Juan wasn't there that day. When Juan lands a punch, it lands hard, and a second or third will put you in the hospital. I wouldn't want even my worst enemy to catch a blow from Tío Juan.

"Stop lying and defend your dad! It's not right for you to be doing this to your dad, Chiquis!" Tía Soco, my father's sister, screamed endlessly. "It's your mom who put all these things in your head! She's the liar!"

Oh no she didn't! Calling my mother a liar? That's when I lost my cool. I grabbed her by the hair and started shaking her until she fell to her knees.

"Leave me alone!" I demanded, choking back tears. "Don't ever call me or my mother a liar again. You don't know a damn thing. Nothing! Do you hear me? Just shut up!"

That's when five police officers jumped in and separated us. They had to escort the Marín family out one door and the Riveras out the other. We were warned that if another fight like that broke out, the judge would have us all arrested. Both families went home that day with heads and hearts bruised and sore. Everyone was feeling a lot of pain.

The verdict finally came after months of anguish, in April of 2007. And according to our attorneys, my testimony was decisive. Tía Rosie's, on the other hand, wasn't quite as strong. When the forensic doctors examined her in 1997, she was already sixteen years old and had been sexually active with her boyfriend. My physical evidence was much clearer, because I was only twelve at the time. It was much easier to attribute the markings on my body to my father. As for the marks on my soul, there is no jury in the world that can measure those.

The judge, surrounded by mountains of documents, called each of us to deliver our closing arguments. Rosie spoke first, and after describing to my father the irreparable pain he had caused her, she ended with these words, which I will never forget:

"I grew up without being able to look my niece in the face because of the guilt I felt. I blame myself for not having reported you when you first did it to me, because then you'd never have been able to do it to her."

I felt an overwhelming sense of peace. Rosie and I weren't as distant as I thought we were at the time. Whatever the outcome of this trial might be, we would remain united. This embarrassing circus was nearing its end; it was time to forgive and forget, and also to offer my own final words. I took the stand.

"Dad, if you had just said you were sorry, it never would have come to this. We wouldn't have needed to go to trial. All I wanted was for you to ask for our forgiveness, to hear you say that you still love me, and that I'm not a liar."

In return, he gave me the most horrible look I've ever seen. His hatred was infinite.

Wow, I thought to myself as I stepped down. *You're gonna get exactly what you deserve.*

Then the foreperson stood up and read the expected verdict in words that echoed throughout the courtroom: "José Trinidad Marín, we the jury find you guilty of three counts of lewd and lascivious acts with a minor child, three counts of oral copulation with a minor child, one count of aggravated assault and one count of aggravated sexual assault of a minor child."

In all, he was convicted on eight of the nine charges filed against him. Two weeks later, he was sentenced to thirty-one years in prison without the possibility of parole or reduced sentence.

A few cries of relief erupted from the Rivera half of the courtroom. On the Marín family side, it was all tears. The court officers placed my father in handcuffs once again.

At the exit, a dozen or so policemen formed a barrier separating the two families. This time, no punches were thrown. Journalists were there, taking a million photos of me. *Great*, I thought, feeling completely overwhelmed. *Now the entire world knows I was abused.*

If things don't go well with Héctor, my one and only boyfriend so far, no other man will ever accept me.

During the next few days, I felt consumed by shame. I didn't want to go out to a restaurant; I didn't want to see anyone. I just felt as if everyone was staring at me, thinking, *Look what happened to poor little Chiquis.* The aura of being the victim really messed me up. My mother's biggest fear had become my biggest torment.

Until one afternoon, some weeks later, when my mother—who hadn't yet figured out how to get me out of my depression—asked me to go with her to one of her concert promo events.

"Princess, let's go out so you can just get your mind off things for a little while. It'll do you good to get out of the house and have a change of scenery."

The look on her face told me that everything would be okay, that there was always a way out of each and every tough situation. And once again, my mother was right, because as soon as we got to the place, fans rushed at me from every which way and embraced me. All sorts of people, from mothers to elderly women to younger girls like myself. At first I felt really uncomfortable and tense, but soon enough the warmth of so many beautiful people began to comfort me. And later that night, the e-mails started coming— hundreds of them, from all across the world. I couldn't believe it! As the months went on, I even started getting letters in the mail from other countries where my mother was already well known. Most of them were from girls younger than me. Many were minors. Their stories were similar to my own and their fears were the same as mine were.

These are the girls my mother was telling me about, I realized. Suddenly, my story didn't cause me as much pain and it didn't hurt so much that the world now knew it too. How right she was to give me the encouragement I needed during the trial so I wouldn't crack under the pressure! Just as she had predicted, my voice was becoming the voice for those who couldn't speak, shout or condemn on their own.

Of the many letters and messages I received, there's one in particular that I remember, in which a young girl wrote, *My mom doesn't believe me*. What a horrible thing. At least my mother believed me right from the start. My mother—the crazy woman who occasionally screwed up and had the damnedest way of expressing everything out in the open—never doubted me. Not even for an instant.

"I'm really lucky," I told my faithful friend Dayanna, who never left my side during those trying times. "I'm not anybody's victim. I have my mother's unconditional love."

"My dear friend, you also have the love of the thousands of women who also believe you. Chiquis the liar is gone," she replied with a huge smile on her face.

Not long after that, I made my first national television appearance to talk about the abuse. Charytín interviewed me on Univision. I would not remain in hiding anymore.

Charytín proved, as she always does, to be an excellent communicator and an even better person. Every question she asked me was compassionate and respectful. And with her respect, and that of the audience, I celebrated my twenty-first birthday that week. I was officially a grown woman.

Around that time, when things were calming down, and because it was such a special date for me, I asked about seeing my father. I felt it was time to sit down and talk one on one, to tell each other what we didn't say in court. But he, by then locked up in the Long Beach county jail, refused my visitation request. His response was that Mikey or Jacqie could see him, but not me.

At home, we held a vote: to go or not to go? Jenni and Mikey agreed: if Chiquis couldn't go, then nobody would. He would see all of his children, or none. But my poor Jacqie had more trouble deciding.

"All right, we won't go," she resigned herself to accept. "But I want to see him someday."

Jacqie's words left my mother feeling undone that night. The fierce lioness trying to protect her cubs just couldn't understand.

"How could they love such a man? They're crazy! How could they still have feelings for a human being who feels nothing?"

Over time, my mother began to understand: that man, with all his crimes and imperfections, would—at least for Jacqie and me—always be our father. We couldn't hate the blood of our blood. We both had enough heart within us to continue to love beyond the sins and the tragedy. It's how she raised us to be ever since we were little girls, because Jenni also had an abundantly large heart.

"Okay, kids, we have to give it some time, but I promise you I'll take you to see him myself," my mother finally consented. "You'll see him, even if he's behind bars. But only on one condition: it's all of you, or none."

For my part, I decided that if my father didn't want to see me, he would at least hear from me. That's just how stubborn I am. I felt the urge to tell him that I still loved him, that I had already forgiven him, but that I had still done the right thing by testifying against him.

However, after my third handwritten letter was returned to me unopened, I gave up. Perhaps the fierce momma lioness had been right, after all.

11.

ON YOUR KNEES BEFORE GOD

In the middle of my father's trial, with the wounds of the past still open and raw, a little episode took place that I've never told anybody about. It's another lesson about the power of forgiveness when it comes to my own life and the lives of those I love. It's the beauty that is born from the guts of even the ugliest and most twisted of things.

The woman who pushed me to "play house" ten years before called me.

"We need to talk," she said, her voice nervous but determined.

"About what?" I answered, confused. Back then, so many things were happening that I was starting to feel dizzy.

"About the most important thing."

My heart froze. Immediately I knew what she was talking about: our secret. The world now knew about my father, but if anyone found out about the other abuse I suffered, I would have died. I don't know exactly why, but somehow this secret made me feel dirtier than all the other secrets I'd had to live with up until then.

I agreed to see her, and the woman came to our house in Corona in less than an hour. I was home alone at the time. My siblings were all in school and my mother was in the studio recording new songs.

When she entered the house, she got down on her knees in front of me.

"Forgive me. I ask and beg for your forgiveness," she said between sobs. Her tears were as plentiful as they were genuine. They came from a place so deep that I swear I've rarely seen someone so broken inside.

Dear God, thank you, I thought to myself with relief. *I didn't imagine this. I didn't dream it up. It also really happened . . . and I'm not crazy.*

"Forgive me, forgive me, forgive me!" The woman wouldn't even stop to take a breath, and her face twisted and contorted in pain. "For all of these years, I've lived with this remorse. I can't take it anymore. I need your forgiveness in order to keep on living."

I didn't cry. On the contrary, I felt very relaxed. At that moment, I realized something that I knew in my heart but never expressed: I had forgiven her years ago! I didn't have even the slightest bit of resentment toward her. And just having her there, accepting her mistake, somehow validated me. It's a shame that the story with my father couldn't have ended that same way: in private, and with the most worthy form of repentance.

I knelt down beside her and hugged her. The embrace was genuine and filled with love, but without drama.

"I already forgave you many years ago. I don't know how, but I forgave you, just as I forgave my father. You can go in peace now."

Her tears began to subside. She stood up, fixed her hair and looked into my eyes with a sense of peace that only forgiveness can bring. She gave me one last quick hug, grabbed her bag and left.

Our time together was that short. No other words were spoken. It was done. Forgive, and be forgiven. And we closed that book forever.

There are some secrets that should remain just as they are, without being judged by men. This was one of those secrets. That morning, we left everything in God's hands. The punishment was the profound regret and remorse, the sort of which I still haven't seen in my father's eyes nearly twenty years after the atrocities he committed. And the divine sentence handed down from above was forgiveness.

I confess that God graced me with an incredible capacity to forgive. Forgiveness gives me wings. It makes me feel warmth in my heart, and it allows me to love the ones I need to love. Anyone who knows me knows this: I am not bitter. Not in the least. I was born that way. Or maybe I just learned on my own to forgive in order to survive.

But the most difficult absolution of my life was yet to come. My most difficult lesson in the art of forgiveness was still pending.

12.

COLD FEET, WARM HEART

"Oh God. My children are doomed to visit their parents behind bars. It's not fair. It's just not fair," my mother wailed, pounding herself in the head over and over again.

Four months after my father went into the system, my stepfather Juan was also arrested and sent to prison. Nobody can accuse my mother of exaggerating to sell more records this time. I swear, drama has followed this family relentlessly. It doesn't just rain every few years, it pours!

"Damnit, Juan!" she shouted. My mother was seriously pissed off. She had only recently been able to sign the divorce papers after three contentious years of separation, and they were just getting back to being amicable and getting along together. And now this!

By this time, my mother was quite an established celebrity, having played to packed houses at legendary Los Angeles locations such as the Nokia Theatre and the Gibson Amphitheatre. And now, both fathers of her children were in jail. One for abusing minors, while the other was caught crossing the border with marijuana.

"What possible reason could he have for pulling that shit?!" I heard her say. My mother was beside herself. While the divorce was dragging on, she was paying Juan $5,000 a month in alimony. Apparently, my stepfather wanted more. He was such a good guy, but he just kept getting himself in trouble. And for that, he was given a ten-year sentence, which fate would not allow him to complete.

Fate also had something in store for my mother and me. The phase of our lives as super friends there in Corona was about to get complicated.

I remember one night when she had a concert in Los Angeles and Johnny asked me to take him. That night, I put on a pair of jeans and a blazer that showed a little bit of cleavage. The show— like all my mother's performances—was intense and passionate. *Only my momma can bring so many emotions to the stage*, I thought as I applauded there, from the first row. Jenni had become La Diva, the lady who owned the stage.

When the concert was over, we went backstage to congratulate her and so Johnny could give her a hug.

My mother was there, changing clothes, surrounded by her manager and assistants. She didn't even look at Johnny. She strode toward me, looked me straight in the eye, and slowly said, "You're not the star here. I am."

She looked disapprovingly at my neckline, spun around on her heels and disappeared into a cloud of fans waiting to take pictures.

Being separated from Juan and the romance with Ferny had certainly brought something out in her. But while there were times where it was fun to have a young and crazy mother, on other occasions, like that night, it hurt.

"Mom is really busy," I said to Johnny. "Come on, we'll see her tomorrow."

We walked away, hand in hand, trying to avoid the hundreds of fans trying to sneak backstage to see her, and we went straight home.

Although I was used to outbursts like that from my mother, that night I had a restless sleep, thinking about what had happened. I woke up the next morning wondering, *Is my mother jealous of me because we're so similar, or am I jealous of her?* But then I thought better of it: no, I'd never felt jealous of her career or of the fact that we were so close in age. I never felt as if we were competing in the same league. The only thing she had that I wanted was her attention. I have to admit that I suffered from that silly bit of jealousy ever since I was a little girl. I always wanted my mother all to myself. I didn't like her being surrounded by dozens of other people, some of whom I didn't even know. I wanted my friend, my sister, my momma at home, but as her fame grew, we saw less and less of her.

People always say, be careful what you wish for. I wished with all my heart for my mother to be a successful performer, and yet sometimes I find myself wondering whether it would have been better to be the daughter of a real estate agent.

The only certainty was that her success was unstoppable. There was no going back, and it wasn't always easy being Jenni's daughter—or Chiquis's mother, for that matter, because I was no saint either. I admit that my love of shopping was out of control, and that really annoyed my mother, who worked hard for every dollar she earned. She was always the saver, while I was the spender. But she was never stingy. On the contrary, she was always super generous with us, our aunts and uncles, our grandparents and even her friends. And I was the one who abused that generosity a bit.

Money was always burning a hole in my purse, and like my grandma, I was more than happy to check out each and every store

I could find. A lot of those silly purchases were made with the company card—Jenni Rivera Enterprises—and that got me into a few problems.

As the person in charge of running the house, I paid the bills and the taxes and made sure there was always money in all of the accounts. I was very careful about my responsibilities when it came to balancing the checkbook, but when it came to whatever extra amount might be left it was *fiesta time*! And whenever my mother would find out, it made her sick.

But my passion for shopping wasn't the only problem. Money attracts a lot of bloodsucking flies, and they were always swarming around the house, smelling the millions.

I see these flies hovering around all sorts of famous people, and personally I keep a close watch on them. All sorts of people are attracted to power and fame, and the level of attraction they have toward celebrities is obsessive. To make themselves feel important, and perhaps even to become indispensable, they start spreading gossip—some of it true, some of it twisted—so they can earn a few extra brownie points from their idol. It's sick!

These toxic voices started popping up back at the house in Corona in the form of friends, employees and even some other relatives who showed up simply to kiss my mother's ass. But the worst would come a few years later, in the new home in Encino, when the flies would be spreading even more gossip and make my mother's last few days on Earth a time of misery. They were the worst thing that could have happened to us.

Meanwhile, the circus back in Corona was growing. New faces were showing up every day, along with new friendships that were not always to my liking. And behind all that, the battles between mother and daughter played out like background music.

I was as hard on her as she was with me. That's just how we

were as mother and daughter: we each wanted what was best for the other, and from that we somehow became two of the most ruthlessly judgmental people in the world.

"That dress doesn't look good on you." "That video clip isn't all that cool." "Don't say things like that, it doesn't make you look good." I hammered away at her relentlessly. I wanted the world to know the same person who I knew: the mother with a golden heart, the honor student, the sweet, mischievous, enterprising woman. But my mother somehow managed to work it so that everything that appeared in the media had to do with this other Jenni: the argumentative, bold and somewhat crazy Jenni.

One Saturday afternoon during a little cookout at the house, one of her friends joked: "Hey, don't toss any beers at Jenni . . . she'll kick all our asses!"

Everyone burst out laughing.

That was just after the time my mother had made headlines in all the magazines. She had hit one of her fans who'd thrown a beer at her during a concert in North Carolina with her microphone.

And there you have the great Diva Circus, with clowns laughing at all her antics. The problem was nobody had the balls to tell her the truth: that it's never okay to attack a fan! Never!

I didn't laugh; I remained serious, and my mother noticed it. She glanced at me, but didn't say a thing. She knew what my opinion was going to be before I even opened my mouth. But I opened it anyway: "Momma, you're a public figure. I'm sorry, but you have to learn to turn the other cheek in situations like that, and not respond with an attack of your own."

"I'm sorry, *mija*," she quickly countered, "but that's something I haven't quite learned how to do just yet. And until that happens, I'll keep doing the one thing I have learned how to do ever since I was little: defend myself, by force if necessary."

My comment had come as a surprise to her, and after all the guests had left, she confronted me in the kitchen.

"Chiquis, I can't be myself when you're around me. You're my worst critic!" she said angrily. "You think you're so perfect! Just let me be who I am! And I'm not like you!"

"No, Momma, you're the one who's always on my case. You nag me about everything!"

Nothing ever came of this argument. We both thought we were in the right. And we were! My mother was my toughest judge. She could ruin my entire day by firing off a single nasty comment: "You've gained weight." "You're always doing that wrong." "So-and-so is taking advantage of you." "You look ridiculous in that dress." And her opinion mattered so much to me that I couldn't live without it. Apparently, she couldn't live without mine either.

That night, we both went to bed angry.

That was around the time the sex scandal exploded: some idiot uploaded a video to the Internet of my momma having sex with one of her musicians, whom she dated for a few months. It was in late 2008, after she had broken up with Ferny and was back out getting in trouble.

This time, I didn't attack her, criticize her or anything. She came home that night defeated and ashamed.

Many people thought it was just a publicity stunt, because that same month her album *Jenni's Hits* reached the top spot on the *Billboard* charts. But the truth was that my mother felt so mortified she wanted to die. This guy posted that video without her permission, and I swear to God, that was one of the few times I've ever seen her that crushed.

"It's gonna be fine," I said, offering her a big hug of encouragement. "Don't worry, Momma." This time it was my turn to use her famous *Don't worry, mija* line that gave me so much strength during the times when I needed it most.

Of course, after the scandal broke, she put her best foot forward, faced the public lashing with her head held high and even cracked a few jokes about it to the media to downplay the whole thing. But behind the façade, Jenni the mother—Jenni the woman—felt like dying. I did too. And needless to say, I never even saw that stupid video.

Luckily for us all, Christmas was coming soon, and Santa brought us the solution to all this chaos: Loaiza.

My first impression of Esteban was, *This guy's a stuck-up asshole.*

The day we met him was cold and dark. My mother was all decked out in a beautiful black dress, waiting nervously for her date to arrive.

"He's a famous baseball player, very attractive. He asked me out to dinner," she told us excitedly.

I was the one who opened the automatic gate and went out to meet him. I wanted to be the first one to get a sense of this guy's intentions. A black Escalade with black rims and everything else slowly pulled around, and out stepped a tall, thin man with a huge gold ring, a diamond bracelet and a massive watch. Very flashy. *Hey, this guy has money. He's not like all the others,* I thought to myself with a smile. Ever since my mother had broken up with Ferny, she had been dating nobodies who were only after her money. Ferny, at least, never asked her for a cent, and was never starstruck by her fame.

Esteban shook my hand, all serious, and I invited him into the kitchen, where the rest of the family was waiting. He sat down, looked at us one by one, and then, with an arrogant attitude, he put his feet up on the table.

Who does this guy think he is? I thought to myself, about to have a heart attack.

Just then my mother came out already wearing her overcoat, and shot him a deadly look. Immediately Esteban dropped his feet from the table and jumped up. He took my mother's arm and quickly said good-bye to all of us. Jacqie couldn't stop laughing.

"If he wanted to make an impression, he sure did. He's so rude!" I said, once we were all alone.

"That guy is a total cock! What an asshole," Jacqie replied, still a bit stunned.

The two of us stayed awake until our mother came home. We couldn't wait to hear how everything went during dinner with such a conceited man.

"He's very nice, very handsome," she told us as soon as she came in the door, before she even finished taking off her enormous leather coat. "He paid for everything. It feels weird not having to be the Bank of America for once!" she joked.

Yes, Esteban paid for dinner that night, and for many others. That arrogant, stuck-up prick turned out to be a complete gentleman, and we all had to swallow our comments. Poor Esteban! I'm sure his nerves got the best of him on that first date. My mother may have intimidated him a bit, and I think, over time, she became even more intimidating.

Days and weeks went by, and Esteban began to visit us more and more often. We learned that he actually treated my mother like a queen. He was very patient, both with her and with us. He never cursed, but what I liked the most about him is that he paid special attention to Johnny, my baby. Johnny was going through a bit of a rebellious phase. Visiting his father in prison was affecting him more and more; Esteban understood this, and disciplined him with love.

With a new love in my mother's life, Christmas of 2008 was looking up for all of us. We had a massive tree, over six feet tall, surrounded by piles of presents. It would have been perfect if not for another case of Rivera family drama: my grandparents announced they were separating. My grandma caught my grandpa with another woman. This had happened before, but this time he had gotten the woman pregnant and there was no turning back from that. The children and grandchildren were all very sad. *Adiós*, four decades of seemingly peaceful marriage. When they signed the divorce papers a few months later, I felt as if I'd lost a huge part of my childhood. It would never be the same, visiting my grandma without the smell of my grandpa's cologne in the bathroom or the pot of beans waiting for him there.

Now it would be a new home with new smells that awaited us. My mother, frightened by the fact that our house in Corona had been robbed twice and tired of driving the forty miles back and forth every day, decided to start looking for a new house closer to Hollywood. She found one quickly, early in 2009, but then it took her another six months to renovate it and make it completely to her liking. During those six months, we weren't allowed to set foot in it even once, until finally, one afternoon in early June, we all piled in the car, and—just as she'd hoped—we were shocked.

"Welcome to Encino!" she exclaimed proudly, after we had passed through two security fences and two sets of automatic gates to arrive in front of a real mansion.

Her initials adorned the wrought-iron doors and were worked into the granite floors. The railings along the stairs were adorned with iron butterflies that she'd imported directly from Cuernavaca, Mexico. On the second floor were five bedrooms: one for every family member. Each room had been designed and decorated according to each of our individual personalities. Needless to say, mine had the biggest closet imaginable. To achieve this, my mother didn't hesitate to have an entire wall knocked down to make two rooms into one.

"It's beautiful, Momma. It's a total dream, just like in the movies," I said, taking it all in as I walked through the vast room with its soaring windows.

But the welcoming party in Encino wouldn't last long. Within two weeks of moving in, my stepfather, Juan, who was still incarcerated at the time, was diagnosed with acute pneumonia. He was taken from prison to the hospital, but in a matter of just fifteen days, he passed away. My immediate reaction, besides the infinite sadness, was one of pure rage! Rage at the knowledge that my beloved Jenicka and Johnny had been left without a dad. Rage because it seemed as if we were destined to never have a father figure in our lives. None of us had experienced that joy for quite some time.

I think my mother realized just how much she still loved Juan during those last few hours in the hospital. She spent his final night there, beside his bed, with Johnny and Jenicka alongside her. My Johnny was crying silently, like a little man, stroking the feet of his beloved dad. There's always been something of an old soul inside of that boy, who seems to see things that others just don't perceive. Jenicka, however, lost control, and her screaming and banging on the walls could be heard echoing throughout the hallways. My little sister has always been Daddy's little princess. It broke my heart to see them so distraught.

The memory of those evenings in Compton, ironing Juan's pants, rushed back into my mind, along with my own tears and pain. I'd bought his shirts and washed his clothes, and he'd always thanked me for it.

"I'll get clothes for him for the funeral," I offered to his family, with whom we always got along quite well. "I know how he would have liked to say good-bye."

I went to the store and chose a pair of white linen beach-style pants, which he loved, along with a baby blue shirt of the same fabric and a white undershirt. Baby blue was his favorite color.

Before leaving for the funeral, I took one last look at him to make sure he looked perfect. Our Juan deserved nothing less. *Oh, shit! I screwed up!* I said to myself. *I forgot his socks! I didn't bring any socks!* Since I'd been told that I didn't need to buy shoes, since you can't put them on a deceased person's body, I hadn't even thought about the socks. But it didn't matter, because he'd only be seen from the waist up in the casket. I kissed him on the forehead and then I let him go. It was time to welcome the friends and family, and to comfort my siblings. I had to console myself too, because life had taken away my secret accomplice, the man who used to smuggle me brownies.

My mother stood next to me, and thinking about her own death, she said, "I never want an open casket. When it's time to go, Chiquis, I need you to be strong and to represent me well. With integrity, and with your head held high. Promise me you'll do that for your brothers and sisters, princess."

"I promise, Momma. But I'm going before you do. I just couldn't stand seeing you go," I answered, tormented by the mere idea of losing her, and forgetting that one of life's laws is that daughters mourn their mothers.

∞

Chinese was all I heard over the airplane's loudspeakers. I was still mourning the loss of my stepfather, but there I was, fastening my seat belt, sitting on a plane to China.

A few months earlier, I'd had the idea of launching a line of perfume under the Jenni Rivera brand name, and my mother had given me her blessing.

"But, Momma, how can I manage all that?" I asked. "Where do I even start?" I had no idea about how to combine spices and floral scents, or how I could ever come up with a fragrance that both my mother and her fans would like.

"Figure it out, princess," she replied, simply enough, with that trademark "you'll manage" attitude that she loved to challenge us with.

"Well, I'm off to Guangzhou, then."

"Guangzhou it is, *mija*."

I think my mother was getting tired of Chiquis the housewife, always depending on others. She wanted her daughter to really sink her claws into life. And this trip to China was, indeed, my first step into the world of business. I had spent many great moments with my mother during her rise to fame, and there would still be great moments yet to come, but that trip was one unbelievable experience. In three short weeks, I learned more about myself than I had in my previous two decades combined.

With my passport in hand, my twenty-fourth birthday just recently behind me and more suitcases than Mariah Carey, I embarked on an adventure where my only option was to return triumphant. The Riveras don't go to such extremes only to return empty-handed. No way. I had learned that lesson only too well, back in the days on Gale Street.

And yet there I was, with my humongous suitcases, completely terrified. I didn't have the slightest idea of how I would handle the language, the business, the customs. I spent that sixteen-hour flight simply crying. *Cry, cry, baby,* I said to myself, softly, as I fell asleep.

"Welcome to Guangzhou!" After sixteen hours of travel, we had finally landed in the craziest city on Earth. And there—with the help of a guide and an interpreter—I made my way through hotels, factories, business meetings and an infinite number of chow mein dishes, until I came up with the perfect logo, the perfect aroma, the complete, perfect package.

With each and every step I took through those streets with that insane traffic, I could imagine the smile of satisfaction on my mother's face—that thousand-watt smile that I know so well.

When I heard the announcement in Chinese on the flight back home, I knew it was time to buckle my seat belt and prepare for landing. In my handbag, under the seat in front of me, was the result of twenty days of hysteria: a perfectly produced and pack-aged box bearing the image of my mother and the logo I'd designed myself, along with the help of the best graphic designers. My first product as an entrepreneur! And from the moment they handed it to me, I knew that my mother would love it. Oh yes. We could argue, we could have disagreements, but we knew one another so well that just by smelling that bottle of perfume, thousands of miles away, I knew that she would like it.

I didn't cry on this flight. And the only words that came to mind were, *Where there's a will, there's a way.* Or *El que la sigue la con-sigue,* as my grandpa would have said.

"Wow, *mija!* You're just like your mother!" my momma ex-claimed when she saw the perfume on her table. She opened the bottle, placed a few drops on her wrist, closed her eyes and took a whiff. Then she gave me a high five and a huge hug.

That embrace was my vindication.

I never turned out to be as good a student as my mother was. I never became the lawyer or doctor she may have dreamed about, but on that one summer day in 2009, Janney Chiquis Marín gradu-ated as an entrepreneur. And a successful one at that, because after that first fragrance came two more for women and two for men, and all of them are still selling like hotcakes to this day. I'd had my fair share of slip-ups and stumbles, but now I had a reason to feel like a real Rivera. No more messing around!

After all the congratulations and the patting on the back, it was back to reality. Or should I say, back to the realities.

For years, my mother had been trying to produce her own television show, and she had finally succeeded. I returned from China to find the house in Encino packed with producers, cameramen and assistants.

"I want us to be the Mexican Osbournes," my mother joked.

"But, Momma, I've read that those reality shows are really bad, that they tear families apart. I don't know if I like this idea," I countered back.

"Chiquis, what I'm trying to do here is establish a name for all of you. With this show, I'll be investing in your future. You'll be earning money and learning the entertainment business at the same time."

As usual, my mother convinced me, and I accepted. I decided I'd do whatever I could to inspire other girls, because at that time, there were no other reality shows about Latinas in America.

We started with *Jenni Rivera Presents: Chiquis and Raq-C*, where I was the protagonist, along with Raquel, a well-known radio personality. Then we released *I Love Jenni*, which involved the entire family. It was harder for the boys, Johnny and Mikey, to get used to the cameras. To me, it seemed fun, and it helped me learn more about myself. But I won't deny that it was a ton of work. People think that reality shows are all peaches and cream, that all you do is put on a lot of makeup, look gorgeous, hang out and talk shit. But the fact of the matter is that a single day of shooting can last eighteen hours or more, and that there's lots of downtime between scenes.

It's a job where you can't call in sick, you can't have second thoughts about it and the stress is exhausting.

But somehow I managed to find a sense of balance between the shows, the kids, the home and the business. My mother was on a world tour, and whenever she came back to Encino, it was to record a scene for the show.

I could feel that Johnny and Jenicka were starting to resent that crazy place. And I have to admit that I also resented the fact that we were forced to share so many private things. I always wanted to save just a little bit for ourselves, but my momma was never afraid of what people had to say.

"We're normal. This is how we are, and we have nothing to hide," she explained. "It's better to be transparent. Nobody's perfect, so I'm not afraid of the camera."

And so, with cameras right there up in the bedroom, Jaylah Hope came into our lives in November of 2009. My sister Jacqie had made me the happiest aunt in the world and transformed the hardworking, disciplined Jenni Rivera into someone as soft as butter.

"I thought I loved my children, but ever since Jaylah arrived, I've found true love," my mother would confess, laughing, totally infatuated with her first granddaughter.

My mother was so crazy about Jaylah that once, when we happened to find the little one cutting up Johnny's passport with a pair of scissors, my momma just told us, "It's fine, let her cut it up. We'll get him another one."

My God, the effect Jaylah had on my mother! I never saw someone so head over heels for her granddaughter.

And with so much happening, we closed out the year: a new home, new projects, the loss of a loved one and the addition of another. The strange cycle of life.

It was around that time that I got a call from Juan's mother, Doña Ampelia, whom I always lovingly referred to as Grandma.

"My Chiquis, I keep dreaming that Juan's feet are cold, so very cold," she said. "I've been having them for months now."

I had to admit my mistake.

"Grandma, it's my fault. I forgot to put on his socks. Please forgive me."

"Cold feet and a warm heart," Grandma Ampelia said, reassuringly. "You loved him dearly, Chiquis."

That Sunday, Grandma Ampelia, a woman of action determined to right wrongs, asked me to take her to the Resurrection Cemetery near Monterey Park, and with her own two hands, she buried a pair of new socks in the ground next to Juan's grave. Amen, Juan of the Cold Feet.

Juan, forgive me for these words. For the socks, and for whatever else we may have pending. I know that my mother forgave you for all that stupid stuff. You have no idea how much we miss you . . .

I love you, Dad.

13.

LONG LIVE THE NEWLYWEDS!

Hey, Ferny, what's up?" I had been sweeping the kitchen floor when the phone rang, and I took the call.

"Nothing, I'm just looking for your mom. It's been ages since we spoke."

"You know she's with Esteban now. He's a good man. You should leave her alone."

"I know, Chiquis. Don't trip. It's all good. Just wanted to say hello."

I kept sweeping back and forth as I listened, a bit annoyed, to the speaker on the other end of the line.

Esteban and my mother had been dating for nearly a year, and they were looking happy and relaxed together. I wasn't about to let old ghosts from the past ruin this great opportunity to have a real man in the family.

"Look, Ferny, you know I adore you, but I'm gonna ask you not to call here anymore." I had never spoken to him like that before, nor had I ever interfered in their relationship, but this time I wasn't about to keep quiet. "Leave her alone. She's got a good man. It's her chance now to be happy and have a real family. Do it for the kids. I love you, Ferny, but it's over."

Dear old Ferny apologized, promised not to call again, and quickly hung up the phone.

I started sweeping harder. Almost angrily. I didn't like what I'd done, but I wasn't about to let anyone or anything interfere with my mother's relationship with Esteban. *Oh gosh!* I thought to myself. *I've turned into my momma, with all her strategies and secrets for protecting everyone.* I felt a bit sad.

The calls did stop, at least to the house phone, and from what I know, he stopped calling my mother's cell phone too.

And soon after that, just like it happens in the movies, would come the request for the hand in marriage.

Esteban was in San Diego training with his baseball team when he called me to tell me he'd be traveling to Los Angeles the next day.

"Chiquis, tomorrow I want to take everyone out for dinner, and I need your help. I want to propose to your mom. But I won't do it without asking for your thoughts first. You're the oldest."

"Yes!" I replied, unable to contain my excitement. "Of course you can have my blessings. You have the blessings of all of us. You're the best thing that has ever happened to my momma. Yes, yes, yes!"

"What do you think she'll say?"

"Oh no. Are you getting cold feet already? Don't be such a wimp!"

We both burst out laughing, and we agreed not to tell anyone. It would be a total surprise.

The next night, at the fancy restaurant he'd selected, Esteban waited nervously until the dessert course before taking the ring out of his pocket. Really, nobody saw it coming! He got down on one knee and asked all of us if we would let him become a part of the family. But all I could think was, *Oh my God, look at that diamond. It's huge!*

Jenicka and Jacqie burst into tears. Mikey and Johnny applauded like crazy. And my mother was so in shock that she kept on eating the piece of cake in front of her. She didn't realize what was actually happening until she saw the ring and yelled, "Yes!"

"Momma, you never had a *quinceañera*. This is your big day, your vindication!" I said, giving her a massive hug.

Later, when things had calmed down and Esteban had gotten up to go to the bathroom, she spoke candidly to me. "I'm forty now, *mija*. It's time to settle down. I'm in a new stage of my life, and he makes me very happy."

Her eyes were shining. Rarely had I ever seen her with such a peaceful glow.

We started planning the big wedding later that same night. The date was set for September, after her summer tour. And we'd be going all out. Oh yes! A wedding worthy of a diva!

Months passed, and to my surprise, nobody consulted with me much about the flowers, the menu or the dress. My mother put her assistant, Julie, in charge of the preparations. I understood that that was her job, but I couldn't help but feel a certain twinge of jealousy. And I got even more jealous still when she picked my tía Rosie to be her Maid of Honor.

"Baby, it's traditional for the Maid of Honor to be the bride's sister. And I don't want you worrying about this wedding. That's why I pay Julie. You just keep focusing on your shows and your businesses. I don't want you to get stressed out."

"But, Momma, it's not that stressful." Of course, it was hopeless to protest.

The more famous my mother became, the less she needed me.

Now, with Esteban helping her with the kids, and with Julie running the office every day, I felt a bit strange. I was no longer the one who bought her clothes, who advised her on her videos or who planned her vacations. My time as Jenni's right-hand woman and the one in charge of the house was coming to an end.

As September arrived, so did the last-minute nerves.

One morning, exactly two weeks before the official date, my mother received a phone call, and she went outside to answer it in private. I knew what was going on from the way she acted, and when she came back inside, I confronted her on it.

"You were talking with Ferny, weren't you?"

"Yes, he just called to see how everything was going."

"Don't do it, Momma," I said, trumping up my courage. "Don't get married if you're not one hundred percent certain. I can see it in your eyes. Don't make a mistake here. You still love Ferny. All this time I thought you'd gotten over him, but I can see you haven't. I know you, I know that look you had on your face while you were talking with him. You still love him!"

"I'm going to marry Esteban. I'll do what I want, and I want to marry him," she replied very calmly, not wanting to start an argument. "I don't care what you think."

"Momma, you shouldn't do that to Esteban. You'll hurt him, and you'll end up hurting yourself," I insisted.

"Don't worry, *mija*. Don't you worry," she said, giving me her favorite line. Then she kissed me on the forehead and left.

The discussion was over.

I swear, all those months leading up to the wedding, I thought Esteban would be the man whom my mother could grow old with. And while it's true that I felt a bit of jealousy at the thought of not being needed as much, I also felt happy. I could spread my wings, start my own family, travel or devote myself to other business opportunities. With Esteban by her side, I felt relief. My mother and my brothers and sisters would have someone to take care of them.

Esteban chipped in money every month for the mortgage, bills and other expenses. He made sure that the children got to school on time. Esteban was both father and husband: the two roles I had played my entire life.

I knew it wouldn't be easy for me to let all of that go, but I was gradually getting used to the idea. Now I could finally start dreaming about my own future.

But that morning, after confirming my suspicions that my mother was not completely in love with the man she was marrying, I was afraid to think about the future. God only knew how that adventure might end. I had a feeling that it wouldn't end well, but I never thought that—of all people—I would be one to suffer the most. This marriage would blow up right in my face and, to this very day, I'm still not entirely sure why.

∞

"Smile for the cameras!" shouted the journalists at the entrance to the impressive ranch right in the middle of the Simi Valley desert.

The big day had arrived: September 8, 2010. There was no turning back. I just sat back, relaxed and prepared myself to enjoy the day with the rest of my family.

White and yellow flowers blanketed the tables and filled the corners of the room. Everything, from the music down to the last detail, was fantastic, and even the speeches given by friends and family were perfect. The bride arrived in a carriage drawn by white horses, and the person in charge of officiating the whole ceremony was none other than my tío Pete, in his role as pastor. Among the guests were people like Joan Sebastian, Gloria Trevi, Tito el

Bambino, and Don Ramón Ayala, who made us dance until we kicked up a cloud of dust. Jenni Rivera wanted the whole world to know that she was a lady with good taste, and she succeeded.

Esteban looked quite elegant, and my mother, in her Eduardo Lucero gown, looked like a mermaid in love. In love with her children, her parents, her siblings. With the hundreds of friends and colleagues who came to join in the celebration. In love with her big moment, with the affection from her fans, cheering from outside the hacienda. In love with life. In love with Esteban, in her own way. My mother said yes in front of God, with all the beautiful and sincere intent of learning to love him more with every passing day.

The problem is that when the heart makes demands, reason is cast aside. There's no room for it in the mind of someone as rebellious and passionate as my mother.

"Hey, *hija,* I don't know what's going on, but I saw your mom on the phone with someone, crying in secret before the ceremony," Esteban told me later, at the party.

"You saw her in her wedding dress before the ceremony?" I chided him.

"I'm not superstitious. I just happened to see her outside in the garden. If everyone's here today, then who the hell was she talking to? Probably that guy Fernando. I've heard about him. I hear the gossip. Even your own mother told me they still keep in touch."

"Oh, Pops, calm down," I said reassuringly, though I knew the same. That call could only have been with Ferny.

Eventually, Ferny himself confessed to me that it was, in fact, my mother who had called him to say good-bye, with all the love that she had, minutes before walking up to the altar.

As time went by, I also realized that I have a confession to make. I have to apologize to Ferny, because I pushed him out of my mother's life, instead of letting them talk. Forgive me, Mother, because Ferny stopped calling for a long, long time, and I know how much that made you cry. Maybe we shouldn't intrude when it comes to matters of the heart. For better or for worse.

"Long live the newlyweds!" the guests cheered.

The last toast to a perfect wedding ended well past midnight. The next morning they began their perfect marriage, and my new reality.

14.

DANCING WITH JEALOUSY

Baby, call him, *por favor*, just call my teddy bear," my mother begged me. This was during the time when I was going out a bit more with my friends. I was learning to figure out what it was like to have a life outside of my mother and the kids. I felt guilty, but part of me enjoyed it. But my mother was uncomfortable seeing me spread my wings. "I'm settling down now," she told me. "And Jacqie is too, with her boyfriend and her baby. When will you?"

"Momma, I'm fine. What's with your obsession with fixing up our lives?" I responded, but my protests were not heard. My mother, as persistent as she ever was, convinced me to look for Héctor, two years after I broke it off with him.

My mistake was calling him, and his mistake was taking my call. And since ashes remain where there once was fire, we started seeing one another, trying to fall in love again. The problem was that our ghosts from the past were suffocating us. In exactly four weeks, we had become the same old thing: I canceled a romantic dinner date because Momma asked me for a last-minute favor; Héctor got annoyed, and rightly so. We spent a few days traveling together to deliver some donations to an orphanage in Tijuana, and we argued nearly the entire trip there. All of a sudden, I saw it all so clearly. We no longer had any patience for each other.

"Héctor, this isn't working out. It's over," I said bluntly. And that's when he gave me his famous phrase: "One day your mom's gonna give you a swift kick in the ass . . ."

That kick was about to come.

As soon as my mother accepted the fact that Héctor wouldn't be fathering her grandchildren, she embarked on a search for a gallant knight. Obviously, he would have to be to her liking.

The first candidate was the boxing champion Saúl "El Canelo" Álvarez.

"Look, baby, I met Canelo's manager and he gave me two VIP tickets to Saturday's fight," she said. A clever ploy. Since I love boxing, I accepted. "He's really cute, young and very handsome. I'll introduce you, *mija*," she insisted, before having me put on a sexy dress and fake eyelashes.

The fight was awesome, and after the final bell, we went into the locker room. *Wow, he doesn't look too bad!* I thought. I was surprised that his face was in such good shape, after his fight. And—of course—he was victorious.

"*Hola*, Canelo, how are you, *mijo?*" My mother got straight to the point. "Look, I want you to meet my beautiful daughter."

Canelo shook my hand. I found him to be very polite and somewhat shy.

"Very beautiful, right? I made her all by myself," she said, forcing the issue yet again.

"Yes, very beautiful indeed," Canelo replied, very gentlemanly.

But, truth be told, there were no sparks from that introduction. We politely said good-bye, and everyone went their own ways. There was no physical attraction or chemistry, no angels playing the harp.

I just wasn't his type, nor was he mine. I don't know why, but I don't like famous men when it comes to boyfriends. It's just one of my things.

The next candidate was a doctor.

"Chiquis, baby, he's Persian, handsome, elegant and he looks like Andy García."

"Momma, I have nothing in common with a doctor."

"He doesn't have any children!" she added with a big smile on her face. To my mother, that was vital. She was obsessed with finding a man who didn't already have a family.

Without even asking for my opinion, she sent him a few pictures of me, and even set up a dinner date for us to meet.

"A blind date? Momma, you're crazy!"

The night before, I sent the poor guy a text and canceled the date. My mother was really bothered by that.

"Fine, keep partying with your friends. You're missing out."

But like in an episode of *The Bachelorette*, my momma found the next candidate quick as a wink. His name was Carlos, and at the time he was the marketing director of Plaza Mexico in Lynwood, the place where my mother wanted to open a sports bar.

"You've got to meet this guy. He's thirty-one, tall, single, handsome, no kids. And he's got blue eyes! Oh my God, I'm going to have grandchildren with blue eyes!" My mom was hallucinating over this Carlos guy. "Look, baby," and she showed me a picture of a blond baby that she'd clipped from a magazine. "If you marry this guy, your children will look like this. Chiquis, you know I can't have ugly grandchildren!"

To make her forget about her disappointment over the doctor, I agreed to go out with Carlos. We went out for coffee a couple of times, but it wasn't going anywhere either. My momma wouldn't be getting her little blond grandbaby. Oh well.

Carlos was gorgeous. In fact, he had worked as a model. A smart, funny and very kind guy. But I have to admit that handsome men intimidate me. I felt nervous, staring into that perfect face. My God! It was like sitting in front of Eduardo Verástegui and trying not to drool.

Carlos called me one more time, but after that he gave up. Maybe he also felt a bit intimidated by me: the famous daughter of Jenni Rivera. That has frightened off more than one potential suitor!

His good looks and my last name—we can be so foolish in this game of love.

But love would—on its own, without any help from my mother—come knocking on my door. Or rather, it sent me a text message: Hola beautiful. Someone gave me your number. How are you today? He already knew who I was, and had been eyeing me at the Billboard Mexican Music Awards. Apparently, we were sitting only three seats away from each other at the theater, but I don't remember having seen him.

It took me a month to answer that mysterious text: Hola. And just like that, little by little, we started exchanging greetings. And then the first flowers arrived. A huge bouquet! Immediately, I called to thank him. It was the first time I'd ever heard his voice. After that, he sent me a picture and I accepted an invitation to dinner.

This guy intrigued me right from the very start, but he didn't intimidate me. I still had some fear toward men. It's a trauma that I think I'll be dealing with for the rest of my life. After the normal butterflies from the first encounter settled down, I felt good just watching him and listening to him.

But the one who didn't feel good about it was my mother.

"Chiquis, is it true that you're dating this guy?"

"Yes, Momma, and I really like him."

"But why, why, why, *mija*? I've heard so many things about him."

"Well I'm going to keep on seeing him. I tried to make things work with Héctor because you begged me to, but that just wasn't happening. Now, I'm making the choice about who I want."

"*Mija*, this guy already has four kids with one more on the way!" That was the part that was killing her. "You don't need to be dealing with all that. There's going to be so much momma drama and baby drama . . ."

"Momma, he's already separated, and besides, there's nothing wrong with having kids. You have five, and all your boyfriends loved you just the same," I argued, trying unsuccessfully to convince her. Neither of us was willing to budge on this particular occasion. No way. I was tired of obeying her when it came to matters of the heart.

Especially since the guy had really won me over during those first few dates. I was totally smitten. I was attracted to him because he was brave, a real man, with his own successful business. He worked in the music industry as well, so we had a lot in common. He was really funny, able to make me laugh so hard it hurt, and he wasn't with me because of my mother's fame. He was just there, sitting in front of me, listening to my dreams and regrets, because he wanted to.

And while I was all caught up being the silly little love bird, the scandal surrounding my brother Mikey broke. The mother of a girlfriend two years underage accused him of sleeping with her daughter. The headlines broke my heart. Mikey's a rapist? I could almost hear the words "Like father, like son" on the lips of every member of the public and the media.

My beloved Mikey is a child of God, and his only sin was to fall in love with a girl who was fourteen when he was nineteen, and under California law, that's considered statutory rape. Having sex with a minor, even with her consent, is punishable by jail time, even though the defendant had just legally reached adulthood himself. During the trial, it was revealed that the girl's mother allowed them to do things alone together like going to the movies among many other places—and that both families knew they were dating—but the law is the law, and this mother wanted justice.

"*Mijo*, you have to pay the consequences for what you've done, but I will always stand by you," I remember my mother saying to Mikey in the kitchen one morning before going to court. Like all members of the family, my mother was both responsible and brave. She never taught us to throw a stone and hide your hand. The Riveras face their problems head-on, and therefore Mikey would face the judge and the media frenzy that surely would be waiting for us in the end.

"I'll always defend you, Mikey. I'm always going to defend you," I said, offering encouragement of my own. "I remember the day you met that girl, at Mom's wedding, and I remember how annoying her mother was, trying to get that girl to sing to the bride and groom. Hell no! The red flags should have gone up right then and there."

Mikey simply replied with a hug, and left for his date with the law.

In the end, they reduced the charges to three misdemeanors, and he was sentenced to one year of probation. The worst thing was that his record would be marred forever, as was his soul, because Mikey is a noble human being with the biggest heart I've ever known. I knew he was scared of being compared to our father.

"You're not like Dad, Mikey," I'd say to him during those dark days. "You're not like him."

And that's how we kicked off 2012: with lawyers and a trial, a new boyfriend and wedding plans. Though it wasn't me who would be walking down the aisle. Jacqie was getting married to her boyfriend after a year-long courtship.

"You can't invite Chiquis's boyfriend to the wedding," I heard my mom say to Jacqie in her office with the door ajar.

"But, Mom, Chiquis loves him. It should be her decision, not yours," Jacqie protested.

"I don't want to hear it. I'm the one paying for this wedding, so I decide who gets to come."

They were talking about my boyfriend! I burst into the office like a bull and confronted my mother.

"You know what, Momma? Maybe Héctor was right. I've never had the balls to contradict you, but from now on, it's gonna be different. I've been dating him for three months now, and besides, it's my sister's wedding, not yours."

"And I don't care. If I'm paying, he's not coming. Period," she said, taunting me by leaning back in the chair behind her desk.

"You don't even know him!"

"Nor do I want to. If you want to date him, go right ahead. But I don't want him around my family or my children."

The gossip had already gotten to my mother: rumors that my boyfriend had connections to organized crime, that he didn't play by the rules and other such lies. Jealousy is always a factor when it comes to the music industry, and if you're successful, to some people, that automatically makes you the bad guy.

"Look, Momma." I was ready to speak to her like I never had before. "I'm a grown-ass woman. An adult. And you need to respect my decisions."

"Oh really?" she said, sarcastically while leaning across her enormous desk. "You're some grown, badass woman?" she continued to challenge me.

"Listen, Mom, I know what you're like. Let's not start a war here," I said, trying to put out the flames as best I could.

"What are you implying, Chiquis?" she asked.

"I'm saying, don't let this get in the way of our business and our personal lives. I love you."

"Don't worry," she said, sweetly, but with that look in her eyes that was always there when she was planning something.

For the next week, we barely spoke to each other, until one day when she sent me a text: We need to talk. Come home.

I'm with my boyfriend now, I texted back, determined not to let her manipulate me, but I was fearful inside.

I don't care. You need to come immediately.

She was so insistent that I started to get even more nervous. I got in the car and headed for Encino.

My mother was waiting for me behind the same massive desk where she liked to play the boss. And that's exactly what she was doing!

"Chiquis, I need you to leave. You have to move out of the house."

"Are you serious? Why?" I immediately felt dizzy and blood rushed all over my body. I had to sit down.

"I was just reviewing some accounts, and look at this: a $3,000 charge at BCBG, another $500 at Bebe. You're spending my money!"

"Momma, every year we do our taxes together and you know how much I spend. This isn't anything new. You've known. I never tried to hide anything. You know I like to shop. And besides, it's not just your money, it's our money."

"Chiquis, I pay you very well. You should be spending your own money on your own whims. Not mine."

She was absolutely right about that. I couldn't argue that point at all. My mother had always been generous with me, but children always tend to take advantage of the situation. Though it's also true that I always worked diligently for her without complaint, and I truly felt that the money belonged to me as well.

"Okay, then, Momma, I'll pay you rent. Let me show you that I can be more responsible. I never stole a penny from you. Nothing was done behind your back. You always knew what I was spending money on, and where I was spending it."

"No, because you're a fucking adult now, remember? Well, now we'll see just how badass of a woman you really are."

"Oh, okay, now I understand! This isn't about my shopping, it's about my boyfriend. It's because I'm still with him." Suddenly it was all very clear to me.

"No, it has nothing to do with him. But since you think you're such a grown-ass woman, then go right ahead." My mother had already made up her mind. My pleas were falling on deaf ears.

"So what's gonna happen with *Chiquis 'N Control*?" I suddenly remembered that we had just started my third reality show, and my mother was one of the executive producers.

"I don't know. I'll have to think about that. For now, the only thing you have to do is move out of my house."

At this point, I simply burst into tears. I just couldn't hold them back any longer. Just the thought of not being able to see my babies every night broke my heart.

"Okay, fine, I'll find another place to live. Just answer one question: Am I still working for you?" I managed to get that out between the sobs.

"No. You have the money from the other two shows, so you can make things work with that. Think about what your next move will be. But, as of today, you no longer work for me."

The next day, I found out that she had removed my name from

all the bank accounts and other legal documents, and that she had hired someone else to take my place.

As I've said time and again, my mother was calculating. In less than a week, she had set everything up perfectly.

Begging was useless: "Momma, please, I'll go to therapy, I'll change my habits, I'll do whatever you want." The mere idea of being away from Johnny and Jenicka was simply mortifying. And she knew that.

With a wounded heart, I found a small apartment in Van Nuys. It was a garage that had been converted into a one-room combined kitchen and living space with a single, small bedroom.

On March 16 2012, there I was: back in a garage. Only this time I was all alone, and without a bike.

I swear, if it wasn't for my true friends, I would have died there. Ellen, Julie, Dayanna and Gerald packed up all of my belongings from the house in Encino and loaded them into a U-Haul. That U-Haul was filled with nothing but clothes and shoes! That evening, I realized that my mother was actually right: I did have a shopping addiction. But I also knew that behind all this was something much more serious than a bunch of stupid shoes and bags.

Too much shopping, a boyfriend she didn't approve of and a dash of jealousy: that's the perfect recipe for mother-daughter drama. Yes, my own mother told me later that same year that she felt jealous of me. Jealous of me as a mother, not as a woman. Jealous because I seemed like more of a mom to her kids than she, who gave birth to them.

Now, with a real husband in the home, her outlook on life had changed. She wanted to cook and take the kids to the doctor, just how I had done, and she felt like a bad mother because she couldn't. All those years on the road and staying in lonely hotel rooms were taking a toll on her heart. I remember trying to encourage her, telling her that a bad mother never would have sacrificed as much as she did for us. Maybe she wasn't physically there each and every night in Encino to tuck us in and give us a kiss good night, but the example of strength that she set was something that stayed with us from the moment we woke up until the moment we fell asleep. To this very day, she's still a presence in that house. She's the love and the energy of the family.

"A good mother isn't always the one who stays home baking cakes, Momma." I remember I told her that once to try and lift her spirits.

And a good mother is also someone who teaches you a tough lesson from time to time. And there I was, doing my work while surrounded by the moving boxes and the mess in my new apartment.

Esteban stayed out of this whole episode. All he said to me, making sure that my mother couldn't hear him, was: "I hope things get fixed between you and your mom soon. You're my daughter too, and I don't like seeing you like this."

At least Ferny would have stood up for me. He would have said, "Jenni, stop this shit."

Sometimes I think that if Esteban had shown more character, my mother would have loved him more. Though I do know that he was fighting for me in his own way. In an attempt to soften my mother's heart, he recorded my niece Jaylah placing one of my bags next to the moving truck, and he sent it to her. What Esteban may have lacked in courage, he more than made up for in good intentions.

Later, Esteban told me that after my mother returned from her trip, she stood in my empty room alone for a few minutes. When she emerged, her eyes were red, and she didn't say a word.

I was never very talkative either. I just lay there on the bed my friends had bought me at Ikea. I didn't bring a single piece of furniture from my mother's house with me. I didn't want to be accused of stealing or taking anything that wasn't mine. What I wanted was to start over from scratch: all new things, and all of them my own.

∞

But in order to start from zero, first you have to hit rock bottom. And I was getting close. I didn't shower for three days, and I left all my damn clothes in the U-Haul parked in the driveway. I missed my babies so much! And they didn't even call me. They were happy at school, with their friends, going everywhere with Esteban. *Oh, they don't need me anymore,* I would stupidly torment myself. *So that's the game now, is it?* I was at such a low point that my own petty jealousy was sinking me, and to top it all off, I kept telling myself, *Chiquis, you have no job, you have no family, you have nothing.*

I sat motionless, staring at open space. I asked my friends to take over. They moved the bed out into the living room, converted the bedroom into a closet and unloaded all the shit from the truck. *Stupid clothes,* I thought. *They cost me everything.*

One morning, after I managed to drag myself into the shower and calm down a little bit, my mother started texting me. **How are you? How is everything?** she asked. I never answered her, so she decided to post a song by Chuy Lizárraga on her Twitter:

Where have you gone, my presumptuous one?
I'm dying for you to return,
I want you to see my tears
They're beautiful, though you caused the pain . . .
Where have you gone, my presumptuous one?
I propose we discuss your return;

Whatever you want,
Whatever you ask,
I have it;
And if what you want simply does not exist,
In that case, I'll invent it.

My mother loved sending us messages through song, especially when words failed her. And since I didn't reply to her Tweet, she finally decided to actually call me. Swallowing her pride, she asked me, very clearly, to return.

"Princess, you should come home. You can have your job back, your room, everything."

Her voice sounded shaky. I could tell she was about to break down and cry, so I got in the car and drove straight to see her. She needed a hug from me as much as I needed one from her.

"Momma, I love you, but I can't come back. Not right now. I already moved out, and it's just not fair. It hurt a lot, and I still need some time," I said, with all my heart.

"Okay *mija*. I love you," she replied, very understanding. Over the years, my mother had gotten more sentimental, especially since she became a grandmother, and she wasn't willing to risk losing any of her princesses. Her greatest joy was having us all there at home.

After that embrace and those words of reconciliation, our relationship felt better than ever.

I focused on managing my finances and expenses better, and I started planning my next business venture. One morning, I woke up in that garage filled with shoes feeling happy: *Okay, this is the life of an independent, single woman. It's not so bad. I don't have to get up early and start taking care of the house and the kids. I can get an extra hour of sleep!* I thought. I have to admit, I liked it!

But what I liked even better was the attention from my mother. She'd call me, invite me to lunch at some fashionable restaurant and we'd sit there and talk about everything, like true friends. Or she'd tell me, "Come over and have dinner at the house," and when I would get there, a place would be set for me at the table. We had finally gotten back to being mother and daughter, not boss and employee. Those few months, from March to July, represented some of the best mother-daughter time we ever had. Once again, we were those two crazy, inseparable girls riding a bike through the streets of Long Beach.

One night, after having dinner with everyone at the house in Encino, I said good-bye and got ready to head back to my apartment.

From the driveway, as I got into my car, I saw Esteban through the kitchen window. The kids were helping him load the dirty dishes into the dishwasher. My mother was laughing as they told her some joke they'd sent to his phone.

"My family is a success, and my life will be too," I said to myself as I drove back to the apartment. My soul was at peace, and I was ready for my next big adventure.

That adventure already had a name. Blow Me Dry: a beauty salon I was about to open there in Encino. I decided to invest what little savings I had in this new project, and to do it all by myself. I chose the place, the name, and I hired the employees. I filed for the permits, paid for the fees and I worked with Iris Corral, my PR agent, to promote it. All I asked my mother to do was to join me for the grand opening.

That evening, all the major Spanish-language TV stations sent reporters there. I was so nervous that I almost threw up. It felt like the first day of kindergarten. And my mother wasn't even there yet! I had to start the event without her and face the cameras alone for the first time. When the interviews got started on the little red carpet, I felt someone tug at my hand. Before I even looked, I knew: *My momma is here.* And the tears started to flow, much to the surprise of the poor journalist who was standing there holding the microphone, trying to understand why I was so excited.

"Wow, *mija*, wow," she whispered in my ear. "You've impressed me. This is so beautiful. But why are you crying, princess?"

"Because I thought you weren't coming," I said, babbling like a little girl.

"I'm right here with you, baby. I'll always be with you," she said, reassuring me as only she knew how to do, and then we walked, hand in hand, toward the new salon and my new future.

The next gift life gave me that strange year came on my birthday.

My mother, Esteban and the kids had invited me to the movies. We went to Pasadena and, although the movie sucked, we had a great time. At the end of the film, someone hugged me from behind. Surprise! It was my boyfriend. But the real surprise was my mother's reaction: she gave one of her mischievous smiles and greeted him just as if he were any other person. I froze, and I guess from seeing the look on my face, my momma decided to offer me an explanation.

"Come on, princess. The two of us spoke yesterday and decided to squash it. We wanted to celebrate your birthday the way it deserves to be celebrated: with a big party."

I swear, I couldn't believe it. That was the first time they had ever agreed to meet face-to-face.

The rest of my friends and family members were waiting for us at my boyfriend's house with tequila and food. While the mariachi music was blaring and the glasses were flying, my mother and my boyfriend snuck out into the backyard while I watched them through a window.

It was time for them to open up to each other. My boyfriend told her that it really bothered him that she was going around believing the rumors about someone she hadn't even met. And she apologized to him, though she added that I was her baby and always would be, and that she would protect me from any and all harm. They kept on chatting for half an hour! I guess they had a thousand other things to talk about that they never shared with me, but at least they were speaking honestly. They were both equally stubborn and straightforward.

Eventually, Esteban came to find me.

"*Hija*, your mom is looking for you."

I went out into the backyard, still pretty nervous, but when I got close enough to hear them laughing together, I thought to myself, *This is my real birthday present.*

"Baby, now I know why you like this guy so much!" my mother said with a huge smile on her face.

"I don't just like him, Momma. I think I love him."

"Say what you will, but he and I have a lot in common. They say girls fall for guys who remind them of their fathers, but you fell in love with someone like me, because I've been both your mother and your father. I always have been."

At that, my boyfriend started laughing.

The party that night ended peacefully, with Esteban and my mother embraced in total harmony, and my boyfriend and I dancing together tightly. That summer promised to be a fantastic one.

But, just like every other happy chapter in our lives, it would be a short one.

I still don't understand what the hell happened. To this day, nobody has been able to explain to me why, in eight short weeks, our heaven turned into pure hell. And the only person who could help clarify that for us is no longer here to tell the tale.

I spent that summer working hard in my salon and planning to start my singing career. It was already a done decision: I was going to make my debut as an artist very soon. It was something I'd always secretly dreamed about, and that was the time to make it happen.

"*Mija*, just wait one more year," my mother said when I first told her my plans. "I want to be your manager, but right now I'm just so busy. Give me a few months, and we'll start together."

Someday, my mother wanted to leave the grueling world of touring behind her, and take on projects that would allow her to stay home and be closer to her children and husband.

"I want to produce an all-female band, like Limite, but with you as the lead singer, princess."

I thought my mother's plan was fantastic. Professionally, between the two of us, there was no jealousy. When it was time to get down to work and earn the bread, Momma and I were a team. And we'd always said that when my mother moved into another stage of her career, it would be to help my siblings and me fulfill our own dreams. "Everything I do is about building a name, an investment you can benefit from," she would say. How many times did I hear her repeat those words? "My dream is your dream," she insisted. But before dreaming about more standing ovations, we had to get Jacqie married!

And that was when I saw the first sign that our blue summer sky was starting to cloud over: my boyfriend would not be attending the wedding. That big show they'd put on for my birthday about peace and love between mother and boyfriend was just a flash in the pan. Once again, my mother refused to accept him as part of the family. She just kept on insisting that she didn't like the fact that he had so many children, that he would never make me happy, that there was something suspicious about him and that he was up to no good. On top of that, I was starting to notice that she was feeling a bit threatened by him. If he bought me a pair of shoes, she'd buy me three. I think that—because he wasn't some kid she could manipulate at will, and he could give me the same things she could—she didn't want him in her life. Or mine.

I was so tired of so much drama that I decided to ignore the problem for the time being and simply enjoy the wedding, whether or not my boyfriend was there with me. But don't even think that I was about to leave him! Eventually, I thought, very optimistically, my mother would end up accepting him. The fight would be billed as Obstinate Mother vs. Stubborn Daughter. And I wasn't about to give up that easily.

As usual, my mother was in charge of the whole party, and coordinated everything down to the last detail. Her daughters never had *quinceañeras*, but their weddings would be the stuff of legend. Jacqie chose Wednesday, September 19, as the day to say the big "Yes." Wednesday has always been my favorite day of the week. My mother and I were both born on Wednesdays, and Wednesdays were our days to get together for dinner and to watch a movie.

And on that Wednesday—the day of the wedding—I noticed a few more signs of the storm that was on the horizon. That morning, while we were all getting ready, my mother told me that she had caught Esteban texting his ex back in Texas.

"Oh, Momma, they have a child together. What did you expect? That they'd never speak again?" I said, trying to calm her down.

"Those texts were too friendly," she replied, suspicious. "But I don't care about that. I'm just sick and tired of all his little lies. Esteban lies about all this bullshit, and it's starting to get on my nerves."

"Momma, there's no way Pops is even capable of cheating on you. You and I both know that," I said, hoping to placate her a little, and I didn't give it a second thought.

I thought it was just the silly suspicions of a married woman. Just like the meaningless twinge of jealousy I felt because my sister Jacqie didn't include me much when it came to preparing for her big day, choosing instead to do most of the planning with our mother, almost in secret.

But all jealousy aside, the truth is that my mother hates lies. Big or small, they're all the same to her. And I think Esteban lied to her because he feared admitting to even the tiniest detail because of how she would react. "*Mi amor*, I went to the store yesterday," he'd say, when in fact he had gone earlier that same day. Or, "My brother invited me out for dinner," when actually it was the other way around. Just stupid little lies that my mother always caught him in.

That night during the party, those little lies and who knows what else they were fighting about were keeping them at a distance. They barely hugged or kissed the entire night. He looked a little sad, and he seemed kind of cold. And to top it all off, my mother was acting weird, but this time it didn't have anything to do with my boyfriend.

Something was wrong in my momma's head and in her heart. What could it be? Amidst the hundreds of guests and all the photos and smiles, I felt a hint of tension in the air. *There's a hell of a thunderstorm on the way*, I sensed.

Something else happened that night that would have lightning-like consequences. Elena, my mother's jeweler, was one of the guests sitting at the table with the new bride. As I walked past them, she grabbed my arm and said, "Chiquis, you're so lovely, you're like an angel on earth. You're the most beautiful girl at this party."

I gave her a hug, thanked her for the compliment and walked away. Elena was so sweet and affectionate with everyone. She was a lesbian, but she liked flirting with just about everyone, just for the fun of it. But from the look on her face, her girlfriend didn't like it at all. She was fuming, which surprised me because everyone knows how Elena is.

That night, the couple danced, arm in arm, to the rhythm of the mariachi music, but the real star of the show was pure, dark jealousy. Jealousy between mothers and their husbands, between mothers and their in-laws, between sisters and friends, between mothers and daughters. Jealousy that slipped in uninvited, spreading throughout the flowers and slipping underneath the white tablecloths. And with that last dance, we all carried that toxic jealousy back to our homes and our bedrooms. Each with our own.

15.

GRABBING RUMORS BY THE HORNS

Sometimes I wonder whether it's the rumors that burn and fuel the jealousy, or whether it's the other way around—if it's jealousy that stirs and provokes the rumors.

In this case, it's impossible to tell whether it's the chicken or the egg that came first. But the explosive mixture erupted less than twenty-four hours after Jacqie tossed her bridal bouquet through the air toward a cluster of single women.

Now it's my turn to tell the how and the why. I hate that I have to do it. Especially since my mother never fully explained it, leaving the episode unfinished.

∞

My mother left nothing written about this conflict in her posthumous memoirs, but after much thought as to whether or not I should talk about what my mother had wanted to keep quiet, I decided to go ahead with it.

From the moment my mother first made this chapter of our family history—which I'm about to discuss—public, on television, and before she mentioned my name as the person primarily responsible for it, the ball was already rolling. I know she meant no ill will, but now it's my responsibility to stop the ball before it rolls any further.

I feel that it is my duty to put an end to these latest slanderous assumptions, and thus to clean the image of both my mother and me. The two of us deserve to be left in peace.

I know that my mother is not here to respond to my comments. I also know that I love her and that my need to talk about this is in no way an attack on her. It is to explain to her, through these pages, what she never let me explain to her face-to-face. I know I have her approval to do so, from wherever she may be, which is also where she will be reading these words. And I know that I have the approval of every member of my family, whom I love and respect.

In this life, no matter how afraid we might be, there are times when we have to face the bull. The bull of truth. And grab the rumors by the horns. You can't say it any better than that.

16.

TOO MUCH SUGAR

There's nothing worse than waking up in the morning with a hangover. And some hangovers, like the one from Jacqie's wedding, can be killers. It came from a raw reality of jealousy and insecurity that you just can't run away from.

With my feet still aching from dancing so much in those damn heels, I took a shower, got dressed and drove the rental car straight to the house in Encino to pick up my brand-new Prius. My mother had leased it, but I was the one making the payments. When I arrived, I found it parked right next to the fountain near the entrance, sparkling new, with the key in the ignition.

"*Mija*, let's go see a movie." said my mother, who happened to be leaving the house with Esteban and the kids.

"Sure, let's go." What a great idea, and this way, I could drive my new car. Jenicka got in with me, while the rest of the family rode in the other car.

Throughout the entire movie, my mother was mysteriously texting someone. Both Esteban and I saw it, but neither of us asked her about it. When we were leaving the theater, though, we learned with whom she had frantically been exchanging messages.

"Elena's girlfriend wants to talk with me," my mother said. "They're having problems. I'm going to go see her."

That seemed strange. Very strange, in fact. Elena was one of my mother's best friends. Why would she want to go comfort the girlfriend instead of supporting Elena, whom she was much closer to? We'd only known her partner for a couple of months, and during that time, she never gave me a good vibe. I don't know, there was just something about her that made me uncomfortable.

"Is it alright if I take your car, Chiquis, so the rest of you can all ride home together in the other car?" my mother asked.

"Will you be gone long?" I asked, intrigued.

"No, no, just a little while. What about you? Will you be spending the night at the house?"

I was surprised that my mother would ask me that. I'd been sleeping at the apartment for months. I loved waking up there, surrounded by all my stuff.

"No, Momma, I'll need to head back to the apartment tonight," I said.

We kissed and she left in my car while the rest of us piled in the other. Esteban was driving with me on the passenger side. Johnny and Jenicka were in the back, fast asleep. It was getting late.

"I don't get it; this doesn't make any sense," Esteban said, not even bothering to hide his suspicions. "Why did she have to go talk with her at this time of day? They're not even very good friends."

"I don't know, Pops. I have no idea."

I didn't want to talk about my mother's issues with him, especially in front of the kids. My mother had strictly forbidden me from doing so.

"There's something fishy going on here. I think you mother's cheating on me," Esteban continued. "Things have been very weird lately."

When we got home, Esteban went straight to the master bedroom. The kids went to their respective bedrooms, and I accompanied them, as always, to make sure they brushed their teeth and put on their pajamas.

My cell phone rang. It was my Tío Juan. He wanted to let me know that he'd had dinner with my boyfriend, and that they'd had a long, man-to-man talk about what his intentions were with me.

"Damn phone. You're breaking up. I get no reception in this house," I told him. "Let me call you back from the house phone."

I had been talking with my uncle for about fifteen minutes, sitting at the base of the stairs, when my boyfriend called. He wanted to tell me his side of the conversation! So I hung up the call with my uncle and started talking with my boyfriend. From what he said, they both seemed to have been content with the outcome of their conversation. That's just how the Riveras operate: new boyfriend arrives, new boyfriend gets interrogated.

"Baby, I'm tired. I'm going to head home, but I'll call you when I get back to the apartment," I told him. Between the two phone calls, I spent about half an hour sitting on the staircase. There were security cameras inside the house that were pointed directly at me. Everything was well documented.

I stood up, took one last peek at Jenicka and another at Johnny and then I went to my mother's room to say I was leaving.

Esteban was lying on the bed, fiddling with his iPad.

"Okay, Pops. I'm leaving. Good night," I said. "I'll just take rental car and come back tomorrow to pick up the Prius."

"I don't think your mom went to see Elena's girlfriend. Something just doesn't look right, *hija*," he said, in a suspicious tone. "I don't know what's going on, but I'm worried." He further continued expressing some of his worries. I listened for a few minutes without saying anything, but very uncomfortable with the situation.

I politely responded, "I don't know." Then, I gave him a kiss on the forehead and left. "Good night, Pops. See you tomorrow."

I left the room and the house quickly. My mother didn't like it when we talked about her and her problems, and I certainly didn't want to get involved in that sort of situation.

∞

When I got back to the apartment in Van Nuys, I could finally breathe calmly. If Esteban and my mother were going to be fighting, I didn't want to be in the middle of it. *They can deal with that themselves*, I thought. And although I missed living with my mom and the kids, it was times like this when I loved my little garage. In there, I was safe from all the fighting, but I hoped Esteban and my mother could fix things for the sake of the kids.

I called my boyfriend one last time to say good night: "Baby, I'm home. Talk to you tomorrow. I'm about to crash." Then I lay down and closed my eyes.

Everything had been recorded, either by my phone records or by the security cameras at my mother's house. It would soon become the most confusing night of my life, for which I would be accused of the most unthinkable of things. And all the evidence I had was good for nothing. When they want to condemn you, they do it without mercy. In this world, the whole innocent-until-proven-guilty thing only applies in cop and lawyer movies.

The next morning, I woke up extra early because I'd promised my friend Yadira that I'd come over for a visit. *She lives so far away, in Victorville*, I thought. *I'd better take the Prius, that way I'll spend less on gas.*

I was halfway to the house in Encino so I could switch cars

with my mother when a phone call from Esteban stopped me in my tracks.

"*Hija*, don't come over here. Your mother's in a terrible mood. She got home at three in the morning and unloaded on me with all these strange questions. She even asked me if there was something going on between the two of us."

"What?" I was so angry that I could barely speak. "How could my mother even think such a thing? Is she crazy?"

"I don't know what's going on, or what Elena's girlfriend told her last night. All I know is that she's on her way to meet with some-one now over at Jerry's Deli." Esteban sounded really nervous. "Chiquis, something's going on. She said she was gonna fire a lot of people today."

"Okay, Pops, thanks for letting me know. I'll talk to her later. Right now, I don't even want to see her."

But before I could hang up, Esteban told me it would be best if I erased the texts we'd exchanged over the past few days.

"No, Pops, I'm not gonna do that. Why would I erase them? We haven't done anything wrong!"

"Because your mother doesn't even want us talking to each other. I didn't want to tell you, but ever since you celebrated the premier of *Chiquis 'N Control* this summer, your mother asked me not to speak to you so much, not to text you, not to look after you anymore. She doesn't want me paying any sort of attention to you."

Bam! This bomb came out of nowhere. Jealous? My mother was jealous? It was true that Esteban was very attentive with me, but no more and no less than he was with any of my brothers or sisters. And it's true that I was respectful and welcoming with him, but it was never anything more than that. It's just how I am with everyone around me.

"No, Pops, I'm not gonna erase them," I refused one more

time. I didn't have anything to hide, and I wasn't going to act like a criminal.

And not only did I refuse to delete those text messages, I actually saved them as further evidence of my own innocence, in case things took a turn for the worse. More evidence that turned out to be worthless when it came time to throw me into the fire.

I decided that with or without my new car—and regardless of whatever drama was brewing there in Encino—I was going to go visit my friend Yadira, just as I'd promised her. Two hours behind the wheel would help me meditate and calm down. I had to think about this one really, really well.

When I reached Victorville, I got the following bombshell of a text from my mother: I know what's going on with Elena. I know you two are fucking.

What the . . . ??? I replied, incredulously. She really had gone crazy! There was no other explanation! She had gone completely insane! First with Esteban, and now with Elena. And what would that make me? The biggest whore of them all?

I called her immediately. I called her time and time again, but she refused to answer her phone. She just kept on texting me, accusing me of sleeping with Elena, saying that Elena had confessed to everything herself that very same morning.

Desperate, I tried calling Pete Salgado, who was her manager at the time.

"Look, Chiquis, I was there this morning when your mother confronted Elena. Elena told us herself that something was going on between the two of you."

"Something between me and Elena?" I shouted back. "Are you kidding me? You're all fucking nuts!"

I couldn't understand any of this. In tears, I called my tío Juan.

"*Tío*, my mom went crazy. She accused me of sleeping with

Elena. She even thinks I'm sleeping with Esteban! She thinks I'm some kind of slut. Please, can you talk to her?"

Juan didn't believe I was capable of such accusations. He knew me better than anyone, so he tried calling my mother again and again, hoping to figure out what was going on with this very strange story. But no, she wouldn't answer him either. My last resort was to ask my tía Rosie for help.

"*Tía*, what's going on?"

"I don't know, Chiquis. Your mom thinks I'm sleeping with Elena too, because she saw my texts, and every time Elena texts me she calls me 'baby.'"

"But what made her even think this?" I asked, baffled. But neither Rosie nor I could make heads or tails of such a mess.

All of a sudden, I remembered the little incident at Jacqie's wedding, when Elena flirted with me in front of her girlfriend. "Stupid rumors and jealousy," I thought.

Tía Rosie confirmed my suspicions.

"Elena's girlfriend got ahold of her phone yesterday and found a picture of you in a bikini from when we all went to Hawaii. Then she went, crying, to your mother about our stupid texts."

Aha! So that's why she was texting like crazy last night at the movies, and that's why my mother ran off to go talk with that girl. It was all starting to become clear now. Her paranoia had poisoned my own mother, and now there were two cases of paranoia to deal with.

"Please, tía. Keep calling my mom. See if she'll answer you, and if she does, tell her I never laid a finger on either Esteban or Elena. Please!" I begged.

But when Rosie did finally get in touch with her, things got even worse.

She relayed my message that I never betrayed her, at which point—from what my aunt told me later—my mother became enraged.

"She found out that Esteban contacted you this morning to warn you about her suspicions, and that made her even more furious. She said Esteban was stupid, that she'd ordered him not to contact your or tell you anything. She's sick of Esteban calling you behind her back and lying to her."

"But, tía, how is that my fault?"

"It's not, Chiquis, but you should give your mother some space," she pleaded. "I've never seen her this angry. I swear, I just don't understand it."

It was at that moment, blinded by rage, that I said the most horrible thing I've ever said about my mother to my aunt. To this day, my words still hurt. But I was so angry at the time that I blurted them out. I just couldn't control myself.

"Okay. Fine. I don't need her. I hate her! I hate her for thinking those things about me! She always ruins anything that makes me happy and pushes me away from her. She's such a bitch! So she doesn't want to hear from me? Well, I don't want her in my life anymore. She's hurting me more than my own father ever did!"

I think my tía Rosie would later repeat what I said to my mother, and of course those words hurt her deeply. The gap between us was growing ever wider.

There were two wounded wolves. And the wounds were growing out of control, aided by all the toxic, gossipy voices surrounding my mother. During those days after the bomb went off, it was those voices—those flies buzzing around her—that were responsible for rubbing even more salt into my mother's wounded heart.

Poor Yadira. My visit wasn't a very fun one. I was on the phone the whole time. The drama was oppressive. I don't even know how I got back to my apartment from Victorville, but when I did, Esteban called me, which further complicated the rumors.

"*Hija*, I want you to forgive me for what I said this morning about

your mother being jealous. It's not true," he said, his voice sound-
ing strange. "Your mother never said she suspected us of anything.
I was wrong."

"What do you mean? What's going on?" Now I felt really shaken
up. "Wait, where are you?"

"Here at home. I have you on speakerphone."

That's when I understood: my mother had forced him to call me
and to deny everything he had told me earlier that same day. And
she was listening in on the call to make sure Esteban obeyed her.

"Pops, I'm coming over," I said, giving them fair warning. It
was time to end this ridiculous nonsense.

That night became another date I'll never forget: Friday, September 21.

I got to the house around ten o'clock that night. I walked straight
into my mother's room without knocking and demanded, "Mom, we
need to talk. Right now."

I was so upset that I was beyond crying. I was more angry than
sad. Esteban was sitting on a couch in the room, just watching us.
I could see the fear in his eyes. *What's he afraid of?* I thought for a
second.

"Okay, talk," my mother answered. Her words were calm but
very cold.

"This is all such nonsense. First, I never slept with Elena. I
don't know who told you that or where you got that idea. We can go
over to her house right now. I want to confront her and I want you
to see it."

"No. We're not going to Elena's house. She's out of my life, and
I have no desire to see her. She already confessed to me everything
I need to know."

"Look, Momma, it's true that she tried to kiss me once. But that
was over two years ago. It's so far in the past that I forgot all about

it. It only happened once, when she was drunk, over at her house, but I pushed her away. And I forgave her, because she's been such a good friend to you, and because I know how much she loves this family. I took it as a simple mistake. And she never tried it again. Not once! We both put it behind us," I explained. "I never said anything because I didn't want to cause problems. But now I see that it has caused an even bigger problem. I'm so sorry." Now was not the time to hide some silly little secret, no matter how pointless it might sound. "I don't know if that's what Elena was talking about, but nothing ever happened between us, and she never tried to make anything happen either. She respects me and she respects you too, Momma. A lot!"

She stared at me, her face emotionless, like that of a judge about to bring down the gavel on an already decided case. But I kept on trying.

"She's your best friend. I know sometimes she makes me feel a little uncomfortable because she sucks up to you so much, but I always excused her because I know how much she loves you. I know that's why she does it. She's the first one there when you're sick; she'll be on the first plane to China if you're feeling lonely over there. Momma, don't blame her and don't blame me. I swear, nothing ever happened between us other than that attempted kiss."

"Well, that's not what Elena told me," she said flatly. "And I have someone here to confirm it."

To my astonishment, Elena's girlfriend then walked in. It felt like all the air was being sucked out of the room as she started talking all this crap about her partner. My mother had brought her into her home. I was speechless. I couldn't believe what was happening. Apparently, after the blowup the night before, she no longer wanted to live with Elena, so my mother offered to let her stay at the house for a few days.

"You don't really know Elena," this girl warned me. "She's obsessed with your mother, Chiquis. I really don't care what's going on between the two of you, but Elena is not good people."

"Look," I replied bluntly. "I met you three months ago. I don't know you. Elena, on the other hand, she's been a great friend to my mother all these years. You? I don't believe a word you're saying."

I warned my mother that she should not listen to this woman, that she couldn't trust her words. But my mother just stared at me with the same, blank look on her face, as if she were some sort of bored judge.

"Mom," I said in conclusion, "I don't think it's right that you're letting this woman into your home and listening to her lies while at the same time turning your back on your best friend and your daughter." And when it came to the issue with Esteban, I looked her right in the face and said, "You think I'm sleeping with him too?"

"I don't think you're sleeping with my husband. It was just a question that I asked him and his stupid ass called you after I told him not to," she replied. Her eyes turned toward him, though she kept on speaking to me. "And if I'm going to leave his ass, it'll be because he's a liar. He lied to me. He swore that he never called you or told you about any of this."

Esteban remained silent. Apparently, he wasn't going to defend himself.

"Look, Momma, don't leave him just because he tells stupid little white lies. Maybe he's just scared. That's no reason to get a divorce."

"That's not it. Our problems are between him and me. He shouldn't be calling you to talk about anything. I'm tired of his shit."

It was clear to me that there was no way to reason with her. So that's how the conversation ended that night, with many questions still floating around unanswered. But at the very least, I thought naïvely, we cleared up the fact that there was nothing going on between Esteban and me. If my mother still had doubts about whatever might have happened between Elena and me, well that was her problem. Oh well. Satisfied that I'd said my piece, I left.

The next day, still very worried about so much drama and so many lies, I decided to visit Pete Salgado at his home. After all, he was present during the conversation between my mother and Elena.

"Pete, tell me truthfully: Did Elena say that she slept with me?"

"No, Chiquis," he answered reluctantly. "That's not exactly what she said. In fact, it was your mother who said it—'I know what happened between you and Chiquis'—and then Elena started to cry and said it was just that one time."

Of course! My mother thought Elena was talking about sex, while Elena was referring to that stupid attempted kiss! She cleverly led her on to the point where she confessed any feelings she had for me, and she hung herself with her own words.

It was a terrible misunderstanding that would end up being impossible to resolve. My mother had already forged her own version of the story in her head. It made it easier for her to think that I could have been with a woman, especially since I'm sure she remembered that little episode with Karla back at the house in Corona. Innocent kisses on the couch had now come at a huge price.

Between the kisses that happened and those that didn't, all of us were caught up in the web of rumors and jealousy that Friday night in September. We were completely tangled up in the most incredible of ways. I don't know if I'll ever be able to unravel it all, or if it even matters anymore. All I can do is ask for forgiveness. That much is still in my own hands.

I can ask forgiveness from my mother, for not telling her until it was too late about the time Elena tried to kiss me. Maybe that would have stopped the rumors from growing so much and spreading so far. But I had learned since I was a little girl to stay quiet. I realized how my abuse still affected me.

I can ask forgiveness from Elena, for the harm that all this caused her. Because of something so silly and so sweet, Elena lost her best friend, and it nearly cost her her career as a jewelry designer when my mother declared open war against her on Twitter. Lots of people stopped buying her pieces. And I also just want to say, thank you, Elena, for loving my mother with all of your heart, and for loving my brothers and sisters with all of your soul. I will never forget that. Maybe, just maybe, some people misinterpreted all your kindness and undying devotion to us.

With the love of my life.

Me, as a baby, about seven months old.

Grandma, Momma, Dad and me at
my mommy's high school graduation.

My third birthday party. The famous green van
is in the background. I loved that thing!

Tía Rosie, Tío Lupe, Tío Juan and me, for my tío Juan's
ninth birthday. He always had me next to him.

Me, Momma and Tía Rosie. I love this picture. This is my mommy!

My family, a long time ago.

This is when my Momma cut my hair and put me on the Zone Diet. That's the thinnest I've ever been. LOL. We were at a Halloween costume party.

A hug I'll never forget.

With my four siblings,
my strength.

My mom having fun in Hawaii.

Getting my makeup
done by Jacob Yebale.
¡Mi baby!

My mom and Johnny.

Me and sweet Luna.

My mom in her favorite spot in the house.
This was the last meal she cooked for Johnny.

My mom with little Jaylah, all of her kids, and my sister-in-law, Drea, who is pregnant with Luna. Our last Mother's Day dinner.

Me and my Momma.

My mom feeling proud at Jenicka's graduation.

My mom being goofy with Jenicka and Johnny.

With my wonderful fans.

At Jacqie's baby shower for Jenavieve.

With my beautiful sister, receiving awards
on my mom's behalf at the Lo Nuestro Awards.

Once upon a time...

...a sweet

little princess

was born...

A twenty-sixth birthday card from my mom. Words I hold close to my heart.

Dear Princess,

Once upon a time a princess
was awaiting to be born and
come into the world to change

a young girl's life. Once upon
a time that girl wondered how
she would raise that princess.
Lead her in the correct paths in life.
She wondered how the princess
would grow into a woman herself
and what kind of person she
would end up to be. Once upon
a time the mommy of the princess
would get cards like this one
welcoming her into the world
21 years later I love how
the story has ended up.
The princess made the mommy a <u>Queen</u> thank you!

...and her family
loved her happily
ever after.

Congratulations
on Your Precious
New Daughter

Happy Baby
To Baby

This is proof that I've always had big cheeks, big lips and a lot of style, even at two years old!

Me looking good ☺.

17.
THE DAY I LOST MY MOTHER

I lost my mother on October 2, 2012. Another date on my calendar. And there's no delete button to erase it from my heart.

My family, her fans and the whole world said good-bye to Jenni Rivera on December 9 of that same year, but I lost her first, on that strange Tuesday earlier in the fall. That was the moment when my pain and mourning began. The heaviest weight I've had to bear thus far.

I remember our final meeting down to the last detail. The clock showed it was nine in the morning. We'd be seeing each other soon in Long Beach, our sweet old Long Beach. My mother had me meet her at a Bank of America, where we kept a safety deposit box registered under my name. We'd kept money and important documents there for several years in case of emergencies.

As I pulled up, I saw her there in her gray Mercedes. My tía Rosie was sitting next to her. My mother and I hadn't spoken to each other since the previous Friday, when the bomb about Elena and Esteban had gone off.

I parked next to her, and I'll never forget the feeling of dread I had inside me. I didn't know how she was going to react. My mother always kept a card up her sleeve whenever she was angry with someone, but that morning she had such a happy look on her face that it inspired confidence. Her hair and makeup looked wonderful, and she was wearing a long, blue dress. I couldn't help but say, "Wow, Momma, you look beautiful!"

"Really, *mija?*"

"Yes, you look divine," I insisted, with admiration.

She replied in her sweet voice, "Thanks. We have a meeting after this; that's why your tía Rosie is here with me."

We waited there for another minute before entering the bank and I told her that I also had an appointment later: an acting class. She seemed to be interested.

"Oh, that's great, *mija*! Is this your first class? You know, I always hoped you'd become an actress. The world of singing can be so ungrateful and demanding."

The conversation flowed naturally, giving me the impression that everything was fine. My sweet mom looked serene, almost tender even. My heart was filled with hope. *Everything will get back to normal between us*, I thought. *Maybe she spoke with whomever she needed to speak, and all those old rumors got cleared away.* There was nothing I wanted more in this world than that.

Once I signed the document to release what was in the safety deposit box, a bank assistant opened the box in our presence. We took out every bill and slip of paper it contained. Part of the money went into my mother's purse, and the rest that wouldn't fit went into mine. When we finished, I had to use the restroom, but first I asked her to hold my bag for me. I didn't want her to think I was trying to sneak anything out.

When I returned from the bathroom, Rosie and my mother had gone out to sit in the car and wait for me. My mother returned my purse, which had already been emptied, and without wasting another second, she simply said, "Okay, *mija*, we'll talk later."

I got in my car and we waved good-bye to each other through our windshields. That's the last image I have of my mother, her looking at me with a smile on her face. We never looked into one another's eyes again. I never saw her smile at me ever again.

The gray car slowly pulled out of the parking lot and disappeared into the traffic of the city that saw us grow together as mother and daughter, and, at times, almost like sisters.

With no idea of what was to come, I actually felt happy that things had gone rather well. There were no bad vibes and my mother had spoken to me again. I was so happy and relieved.

That night I went to dinner at Corky's BBQ with my friend Dayanna. I wanted to tell her how excited I was after meeting with my momma. We sat down in a booth, and no sooner had I ordered my Coke than my phone beeped. I had just received an e-mail from my mother with a subject line that read "Lights On."

In the ten neatly written lines of that e-mail, she officially accused me of having been in bed with her husband, and that she knew this for a fact. She went on to describe, in detail, how and where we had our encounter: the previous Thursday, at the house in Encino after the movie, while she was out talking with Elena's girlfriend, in her bedroom closet. In capital letters, she let me know in no uncertain terms that I was out of her life forever. At that point, I couldn't even finish reading it. I slammed my phone down on the table and began to cry. What began as a rumor between a couple of old fools was quickly becoming something much more sinister, something monstrous!

"Sister! Are you okay? Dayanna asked, astonished.

"No. I don't know. My mother went crazy. I don't know what's going on. I need to get out of here, please."

We put a twenty-dollar bill on the table and ran off.

Ever since that day, whenever I drive down that street and see that restaurant, my stomach twists into knots. It hurts me to the core.

From there, we went straight to the house in Encino. That level of accusations and pain needed to be resolved face-to-face. But when we got there, I discovered—much to my surprise—that all the locks and key codes had been changed, and nobody was answering me on the intercom. I got down on my knees in the middle of the driveway, right in front of the iron gate. I cried, I shook, I wept. What was going on? It was the most twisted nightmare a daughter could ever imagine.

I called my sister Jenicka. She didn't pick up. My siblings had already been warned, and I'm sure my mother had ordered them not to speak to me. Eventually, Jacqie took my call, and I asked her, "Jacqie, did you know about this?"

"Yes, sister. I've been praying since yesterday. I didn't know what else to do."

Just the previous day, Jacqie and I had spent hours looking for dresses for Jenicka's *quinceañera*. Hours of shopping together, two good sisters and friends, talking and laughing.

"Why didn't you say something to me? And do you really think I actually did that?"

Her answer killed me yet again. It was another stab directly into my gut.

"Yes, sister. Yes, I do."

"What???" I screamed. I couldn't even go on. I felt so angry and confused that I just hung up.

If my sister thought I was capable of such a despicable thing, then everyone would. The key was to find a way to get in touch with my mother and talk directly with her. She was the only one who could get me out of this mess.

I asked Dayanna to take me to my grandmother's house in

Lakewood. Eventually, my mother would have to go there to pick up Jenicka.

Damn those L.A. freeways! It seemed like it took an eternity and a half, but finally we reached my grandmother's street and parked around the corner from her house. From there, I called my tía Rosie. I didn't want to barge right into my grandma Rosa's house and concern her with all this drama. Rosie answered on the first ring, but she asked that I just give my mother some time. It wasn't a good idea to see her right now, she said. Clearly, she knew about everything, and clearly she was involved in that little scheme that my mother put on at the bank earlier that same day, pretending that everything was fine.

From my vantage point, I saw the gray Mercedes drive past. It was a cold gray. Not shining like it was that morning. We didn't dare follow it. My mother had made it very clear that she didn't want to talk with me, let alone see me in person. She parked right at the front door, and like a flash of lightning she was in and out with Jenicka in hand. She left without ever seeing me there, without giving me so much as a second to hug her, like I wanted to do, as a means of explaining that I could never do such a horrible thing. Never! Esteban never looked at me with anything other than the eyes of a caring stepfather. Ever!

That night, my mother changed her phone number and e-mail address. But before that, she sent me another round of horrible messages. Words that I haven't been able to delete from either my computer or my heart. Words that still haunt me in my dreams. For a moment, I thought about calling Esteban. He'd been in similar situations, and worse. Surely he would understand.

My tía Rosie had told me that, after the huge fight we all had at the house on that Friday, Esteban had gone down to San Diego to spend some time with his parents until the storm passed.

Dayanna grabbed my arm and stopped me before I could dial my phone.

"No, Chiquis, don't make it worse," she said with all the love of a dear friend. And she was right. Talking with Esteban would just make my mother even more angry.

Poor Esteban. I, more than anyone, know how much he loved my momma. But fear stopped me from calling him. Better to not push him on this. He was an intelligent man and I trusted that he could take care of himself.

In the midst of all the fear and anguish, the only thing that was clear to me on that night of October 2—as I closed my eyes and drifted off to sleep, exhausted by all the drama—was that Esteban had lost the love of his life, and I had lost mine. A daughter is bound to her mother by a lifetime of stories, and the love she has for her is a truly great love. In fact, it's the greatest love.

When I woke up the next morning, the first update I got was from my mom's secretary Tere. The meeting my mother had told me she had after our meeting was, in fact, with Esteban. It was a calculated joint meeting, just as mine was.

That same afternoon of October 2, Jenni Rivera, wearing her beautiful blue dress and her finest makeup, said good-bye to me in Long Beach, drove down to San Diego, and, in front of the entire Loaiza family, she personally served divorce papers to the man who—until just a few days prior—had been the perfect husband. Almost perfect. Esteban's divorce proceedings started on that day, and so did mine.

The next surprise would come later that afternoon. In her weekly radio show, *Contacto Directo con Jenni*, my mother said—very calmly and matter-of-factly—that she had filed for divorce from Esteban, and that she wouldn't be giving any further details because the reasons were so awful and she didn't want to hurt my grandma Rosa, who adored her son-in-law so much.

With that announcement, the fuse had been lit, and there was no way to put it out. However, the worst bomb of all—the one the media would set off—had yet to detonate. That would be the bomb that would destroy me too.

Amid all the explosive news, I almost forgot that it was October 3: Jenicka's birthday! We had planned a little get-together for that evening. I kept telling myself, *You have to go; you owe it to your sister.* In a moment of innocence, I even imagined that maybe my mother hadn't told anyone outside the family about her horrible suspicions regarding Esteban and me, and that perhaps I could enjoy the party as just another guest.

The party was to be at a bowling alley in Studio City after the radio show.

I went by myself, putting on the best face that I could. I remember walking into the place and seeing the whole family looking super happy and more united than ever.

My mother didn't greet me. Her friends ignored me like a shadow. It was obvious that everyone knew. I tried to stay on my feet, but my head was reeling. I felt awful, monstrous even, but I promised to be strong for Jenicka's sake.

Jacqie seemed to be the only sibling present. My mother and Jenicka spoke only to her. I started to wonder whether Jacqie enjoyed my times of stress, and was happy to command all of my mother's attention. Maybe I'm wrong. I love Jacqie, but at that moment, there were all sorts of strange feelings that seemed to be taking over me. I felt like the girl at school who got trapped in a corner by all the other kids. I was now the outcast.

Obviously that was not the time to try and seek justice, so I decided to leave the party early with a polite smile and a good-bye that no one seemed to hear. But at least I was able to give Jenicka a big hug and wish her happy birthday. It was well worth all the humiliation for me to do that for Jenicka.

Three days later, I would have to face scorn and rejection yet again. And that time, there was no escape. On October 6, the long-awaited *quinceañera* was celebrated. Jenicka would be the first of the sisters to celebrate it with a real party, just like the rest of us had always dreamed of. I couldn't miss it. Plus, my sweet little Jenicka still wasn't aware of the extent of the family drama. All they told her was that Mom and Chiquis were mad at each other. Nothing more.

That Saturday, I got up and worked up some courage. I put on a golden skirt and a salmon-colored blazer: the official party color. I was in no mood to wear a gown. And just like that, clad in those sweet tones, I went, alone, to the slaughterhouse.

I felt so small and vulnerable! Like a huge weight was crushing my chest. My knees were shaking and the whole way there I wanted to turn around. How had I gone from being my mother's right-hand woman to the most hated member of the entire Rivera family?

I walked into the hotel where the religious ceremony was about to begin. Upon direct orders from my mother, I was forbidden from bringing any guests, and even a few of my friends had been disinvited via a scathing e-mail she had sent the night before.

As soon as I entered, Vanessa, one of my mother's closest friends, looked at me with such hatred in her eyes that I thought she was going to choke me. Other people who always used to greet me were now ignoring me completely.

My mother entered through a different door, also alone, in her new role as the recently separated woman, and sat down near the front. Nobody asked her about her beloved husband. Friends and acquaintances alike seemed very well informed about the new family order. At this point, everyone also knew that I was marked with the proverbial scarlet "A" on my forehead.

Even with all this tension in the air, I felt obligated to sit in the same pew as my mother, as we had planned in the rehearsals. Together, and yet so very far away from each other. Sitting seats away from each other, but with miles between our two hearts.

The ceremony began, and soon came the time where I would have to get up and walk down the aisle under the scrutinizing eyes of everyone. I had promised that I would give the speech celebrating the passage from girl to woman and place the crown on Jenicka's head. It meant so much to me. I'd spent days preparing those words for my beloved sister. It was her big moment.

When I got to Jenicka and stood next to her, I was stunned. Frozen. I imagined that once I started speaking, everyone would break into cruel laughter. That the whole crowd was backing my mother. Everyone on the side of the great Jenni! She was the one with the money and the power. It was more convenient to go along with the great Diva and to hate me, even without knowing the details. I felt so betrayed by everyone.

Despite feeling overwhelmed by fear, I managed to break my silence and say a few words. I couldn't remember the speech I had memorized, so instead I improvised a few lines, offering good wishes of love and affection for my sister. For better or for worse, one of the most terrifying moments of my life was over relatively quickly. I turned around and went back to my seat. My face was burning. My mother was just two steps away from me, in the same row, but not once did she turn her head. She never even gave me the slightest glance. It was like sitting next to an iceberg or a steel robot. There were no feelings at all emanating from her, and I felt myself sinking deeper and deeper into that torturous chair.

The only people who sat and spoke with me for the rest of the entire night, including dinner and dancing, were my tío Juan and my tía Brenda. Juan insisted that they should give me a chance to explain my side of the story. He was the only one who had the balls to go against my mother's wishes and tell her to calm down.

"I'm not taking sides one way or the other," he said, trying to explain it to my mother. "I just want to fix the problem."

But his words would fall on deaf ears. Between the music and the laughter, nobody heard him.

As the night was coming to an end, my mother went to change clothes. When she returned to the ballroom, there were only three or four of her friends still there. She sat down with them and poured a round of shots. After their drink, she burst out laughing. I know that laugh. She was acting. Her real laugh was joyful and mischievous. Even today, I can hear it in my heart. But that laugh—the last one I would ever hear—was the one she used when she was furious but wanted to hide it.

Nothing more to do here, I thought, so I turned around and left.

Outside on the hotel steps, the night was getting cooler. Halloween was coming up soon and a chill was in the air. It seemed to take forever as I waited for the valet to bring my car around.

My tío Juan came over and gave me a hug. He was also leaving the party. Just then, the gray Mercedes blew past us. My mother was behind the wheel, with her eyes focused straight ahead, and Johnny and Jenicka were with her. None of them turned to look at me. Not one.

That was the last time I saw my mother alive. On the night of October 6. Her salmon-colored dress—which was the color Jenicka had chosen for her party—is now on display at the Grammy Museum. It was brought there, some months later, by the whole family, during a small ceremony in her honor. Who would have thought it, the last dress in which I'd ever see her walk, dance or raise a toast.

The next day, after the nightmarish *quinceañera* was over, I got another one of her crushing messages, delivered via a family member: do not come by the house anymore. There was a restraining order against me, and I was not allowed to see Jenicka, Johnny or even Mikey anymore.

In desperation, I turned to Twitter. How else could I contact her? I didn't have her new phone numbers. "Please, Momma, listen to me, I love you and I need you to hear me." I sent this as a direct message, of course. And of course, there was no reply. Soon after, she blocked me.

My private pain was about to become public. Social media, magazines, television. Now, it wouldn't be just my mother and my family who hated me. Now the world would hate me as well. *Good luck, Chiquis*, I thought, trying to encourage myself. *You overcame the ordeal with your father and you can overcome this*. I knew what was coming: the comments, the criticisms and the scorn. And I would face it all with dignity, just as I had before. Just as she had taught me to do.

I was left with the task of understanding how my mother came to the sickening conclusion that Esteban had cheated on her with me. I could understand the bullshit with Elena: the attempted kiss, the compliments and the jealousy of that clown of a girlfriend she had. But Esteban? Who could have invented the filthiest rumor of all? How? I had to find the answer . . .

18.

SOMETIMES YOU HAVE TO BE CRUEL . . .

I started to pray with your tía Ramona and I asked God to give me a sign," my grandma told me over the phone. "And I know that you didn't do it, because I feel a great sense of peace in my heart. That is the sign. Just give your mother some time, *mija*."

My grandma Rosa was one of the few who didn't believe everything was that was being said out there. She's a woman of instinct and faith, and both of those indicated to her that neither Esteban, nor I, were capable of such things.

"But why can't you convince my mother that she's wrong?" I begged her.

"Because she doesn't want to talk about it. She would fly into a rage. You know how your mom can be." And with that, my grandma broke down crying.

I calmed her down and promised her that I would go see her just as soon as I could. Though the truth was that I didn't even have the courage to leave my apartment. And why would I? Talking to another Rivera would only cause more harm. Some of them weren't even speaking with me.

Tía Rosie would still call me from time to time, but she was more playing the part of a good sister than a good aunt. Her words were comforting, though from afar. She took on the role of referee between mother and daughter—always a scary proposition.

My mother even warned her, "You're either with me or against me." Rosie was walking on eggshells and she knew it. Everything was black and white as far as my mother was concerned. There were simply no gray areas.

"No, Chiquis, I don't feel that you did such a thing. My heart tells me now, but you have to understand my situation. She's my sister, one of the people I love most in my life." With these words, my aunt made it clear that—although she wasn't going to condemn me—she wasn't going to throw me a lifesaver to rescue me either.

And I was drowning. Slowly. Very slowly. Drowning alone, trapped in that tiny little garage.

My tío Lupe was having his own problems with my mother around that time, and they weren't speaking. He encouraged me to fight for my innocence and suggested I take my version of the story to the media.

"No, tío. You're crazy," I replied. "The world doesn't know that my mother accused me of sleeping with her husband. All they know is that they're getting a divorce. That's it. Bringing that part of it up would be suicide!"

"That may be, Chiquis, but knowing your mother, everything will come out sooner or later."

Tío Lupe had his doubts, but to me it was clear: bringing everything to light was deadly poison. Poison that someone else was going to provide me with.

One morning, determined to exhaust all my options, I went to see my tío Pete at his office on Market Street in the old Long Beach neighborhood. Rosie was waiting there with him.

"Let's run a lie detector test," my uncle suggested. In fact, there were many members of the Rivera family who were feeling desperate and who wanted to cure this cancer that was eating away at our family.

"Are you willing to take one?" he asked. "I'll find an expert to administer the test and I'll pay for the costs."

"Yes, of course! Tell my mother to send us an e-mail with the questions she wants answers to, and I'll answer them all, in front of the machine and in front of you all," I replied without hesitation. "I have nothing to hide and nothing to fear."

A few minutes later, instead of receiving a list of questions from my mother, what we got was a text sent to my tío Pete's phone. It read: TELL HER SHE NO LONGER HAS A MOTHER. FORGET ABOUT ME. AND PETE, IF YOU WANT TO BELIEVE HER, THEN GO AHEAD AND BELIEVE HER. I DON'T NEED ANY MORE FAMILY, AND I DON'T NEED A LIE DETECTOR TEST.

With tears in her eyes, Rosie said to me, "I'm afraid to admit it, but I think my sister has gone crazy. She just told me to throw a Bible at your face, and that if you don't accept what you did, you'll never be able to enjoy God's blessings in this life."

"But how can I admit something I didn't do? That's a sin! That's lying to God!"

"I know, Chiquis. I just don't know what to do. I don't want to lose her. I wouldn't be able to live without her. The day she wasn't speaking to me I was devastated. And that was only one day."

"But what about me? I have to live without her and my brothers and sisters for the rest of my life?"

"I know, baby. I'm sorry. All I ask is that you give her time. I'm sure the wounds will heal eventually. I'm begging you, just be patient."

I'll never forget that moment between my aunt and me. That

bittersweet moment. I could feel all her love and her desire to protect me. However, at that moment I knew that she wasn't going to go to bat for me the way I had gone to bat for her many years ago during the trial against my father. It went against my heart to testify, but Rosie and my mother begged me to do it to bring Rosie peace and justice, which I felt I was being denied of in this situation. I was disappointed and very much alone with nobody taking the stand for me.

And that's when it dawned on me: I wouldn't be winning this battle with the help of any family members.

I left Tío Pete's office seeing things more clearly. Nobody was going to bite the hand that fed them. And they're not to blame. Jenni Rivera was the one who financed everything. I saw for myself the monthly donations my mother made to Tío Pete's church, of which my tía Rosie was also a part. Envelopes with twenty, forty, even sixty thousand dollars at a time, which I sometimes delivered in person. My mother, like any good daughter, took care of all my grandma's expenses, as she did with everyone. And I can't criticize them for it, but this makes for a complicated relationship. At some point, she's not just their sister. She's their boss. And I couldn't compete with the boss.

The only one who didn't seem to be intimidated by his sister, again, was my tío Juan, but there was little he could accomplish on his own. He begged me to just forget about it, to keep moving forward, and not to expect anything from anyone.

"Chiquis, here's the situation," he said to me that same night, trying to open my eyes. "Your tío Pete thinks that you did betray your mother with Esteban."

I asked, "Why? How? What do you mean?"

"He said just by looking at you he could tell. Don't waste any more of your time talking to him."

Sadness flooded me to the core. Were those the judgments of a man of God? Of a pastor? With those words, my tío Pete had thrown the stones that the Pharisees didn't even dare to hurl at Mary Magdalene. He had condemned me as just another prostitute in a matter of seconds. And unfortunately, I didn't have Jesus with me to draw a line in the sand.

Even so, I love my tío Pete a lot, and I know he's a good man. He just got caught up in the circumstances, like so many others did during those days of contagious madness. And eventually he would sit down and listen to me, and he came to see that I was not guilty of such a terrible sin.

But for that month of October, there was no Jesus and no solace for me. The next flying stone to hit me in the head was thrown directly by my mother's hand, but it didn't hurt, because money was the least of my concerns.

It was October 12. Columbus Day. The Day of Disinheritance.

The legal proceedings to remove me from my mother's will had been finalized, with a simple amendment to the original document she had prepared just months earlier.

"I exclude you to assure myself that, if you decide to kill me, you will not receive a single cent after my death." Those are the words that my mother communicated to me through my tía Rosie.

Kill her? How could she think I was capable of doing such a thing? A daughter killing her mother over an argument based on nothing but rumors? No, these words were clearly directed toward my boyfriend. Since my mother always believed the rumors that he was some kind of a mobster, I'm sure it crossed her mind that he could be capable of such a barbaric act. *She really has gone crazy*, I thought at that moment. There really was no other explanation.

With that as the backdrop, I started to forget about the Riveras, as they did me. Said and done. Over the next few weeks, Tío Pete stopped replying to texts. Understood. Rosie took longer to return calls. Message received. Chiquis was officially excluded. Chiquis had been forgotten.

The saddest part of this whole convoluted story is that everyone was so afraid of losing their sister that nobody would so much as lift a finger to help me. And two months later, we lost her forever. We all did.

Sometimes I wonder if God sends us hidden messages but doesn't give us time to understand them until it's too late.

Once I resigned myself to the fact that none of my aunts or uncles were willing to help open the door for me back into Encino and into my mother's heart, I lay down on the bed in my tiny little apartment and I didn't get up for days. I fell into a deep depression. I went for what seemed like ages without speaking to my siblings. Mikey secretly came to see me once with his girlfriend, but was always afraid that he'd get caught. From my dear Jacqie there wasn't a peep. That was the most disappointing thing to me. Jacqie was twenty-three, she was married, she was an adult who could make her own decisions, and she could have come to help me or console me if she'd wanted to. But she didn't. If she had confessed to killing someone or committing some other horrible crime, I would have embraced her. I wouldn't have pushed her away.

Jacqie slammed the door in my face. She did that to me, the sister who always got her out of trouble in school or saved her butt a thousand times at home. Without getting too much into it, I was the one who had helped her break the news to our mother that she'd gotten pregnant. Every time Jacqie needed someone to stand up for her, I was there. I was always willing to do that, and I would have willingly given my life for her, if that had ever been necessary.

Instead, Jacqie decided to totally take my mother's side, and enjoy her time playing the part of the oldest daughter.

Jacqie and Jenni: the new dynamic duo. I admit, I was very jealous. I couldn't help it. The difference is that God gave me the opportunity to get my Jacqie back and regain her trust. And for my part, she regained all of the love that I had for her. When it came to my mother, on the other hand, destiny had something else in store for us.

∞

One afternoon, lost between the jealousy and solitude that had taken over my life, I felt like I'd hit rock bottom. Suddenly, I remembered the two handguns that were still in my possession, since someone had broken into the house in Corona. My mother was so scared that she insisted I learn to shoot and got me a permit. She bought the guns herself and hid one at each end of the house. She was worried about leaving us alone on that hill, with no neighbors nearby. But now I was the one who was worried, because these guns were within reach, and I told Dayanna I was having crazy thoughts. I was losing my will to live. My friends— my only supporters during that time, along with my boyfriend— scrounged around every square inch of that apartment until they found the two guns, and they took them away from me. Gerald and Dayanna were so concerned about me that they wouldn't leave me alone for even a moment, let alone when there might be weapons around. That was the first time in my life when such a thought even crossed my mind. With everything that I'd been through in life, that was only time that I ever thought death might actually be better.

Those October nights were my nights of terror. But the real horror would come to me in a magazine.

Up until that point, the world remained oblivious to my drama, my exile and my depression. Jenni Rivera Will Not Discuss the

True Motives Behind the Divorce, the headlines simply said ever since she announced her divorce from Esteban.

Hmmm . . . My mother is being very discreet with the media, I thought.

But that discretion lasted a mere twenty days. Just until October 23, when "somebody" leaked the true family drama to *TVNotas* magazine. As they say, the shit hit the fan, and we all ended up getting splashed.

According to the magazine, "Jenni filed for divorce because she caught Esteban stealing money and having sex with her daughter." Me! When I read those words on the Internet, it felt like fatal poison coursing through my veins. *And there you have it. My true agony can now begin*, I thought. I tried to find an upside to it, but there wasn't one.

The publication cited a mysterious source close to my mother: in other words, one of those toxic voices that was constantly buzzing around her, telling her that Esteban had financial problems. It said that my mother noticed money missing from her accounts and that she installed a camera to try and see whether he was the one who was stealing from her. According to her, she saw Esteban stealing cash on camera, and later she saw the two of us leaving the bedroom, fixing our clothes in some suspicious manner. For the love of God! What outrageous, horrific accusations!

Is that alleged recording from the night she left us with the children after the movie? Ridiculous! I was in the bedroom for not even five minutes, and that was to say good-bye! I had proof that I was sitting on the damn stairs the entire time, talking to my uncle and my boyfriend on the phone!

Who? Who could have said all those things to *TVNotas*? If my mother wanted to remain silent—which is what she stated in the only interview she gave to the media about the divorce—then whoever this whistleblower was had really messed up. That much was clear, unless my mother, deep down, really didn't care about keeping it a secret.

I have a pretty good idea about who opened her mouth. What I'm not quite as sure about is what they stood to gain by doing it. Elena's ghost had come back to haunt me once again.

Instantly, my phone began ringing and vibrating like crazy with tweets, texts, messages and e-mails. They were rolling in by the dozens! Within a matter of minutes, my in-box and social media pages were flooded with the most horrible insults I've ever read, and which I'll never read again (because now I just delete such things outright). "You fucking whore. How could you do that to Jenni? I hope you die." That was one of the kinder ones that I remember.

At first, I made the mistake of answering a few of them. I thought it was only fair. I defended myself. But soon enough, I realized that it was useless. My words only added more fuel to the fire. So I stopped completely. What a feeling of powerlessness to hear all these atrocities and not be able to proclaim my innocence to the world!

But, leaving the disgusting tweets and haters aside, my immediate concern was for my mother. It wouldn't take her long to respond. Would she deny these allegations or come out with her guns blazing to give me the final death shot?

The first ones to start launching missiles were the paparazzi. They started to follow me everywhere, and would even station themselves outside my salon for hours, waiting for me to appear.

"If they can find you, some crazy fan could find you too. Someone could follow you home one night, and who knows what they might do!" my publicist, Iris Corral, said.

Iris was truly alarmed. As a professional, she'd never seen

such aggressive bullying. Neither of us took the messages "I hope you die" or "You deserve to die" lightly.

She advised me not to go to the salon for a few days. I really wasn't in the mood to work, but it was—and is—my business, and I was handling it personally.

Thanks to my fabulous team, led by my manager, the salon was able to stay open and do business as usual, despite the swarm of photographers camped out on the sidewalk.

During that time, Iris became my constant, inseparable friend. I was already accustomed to facing the public, being the daughter of La Diva, but this time was different. I couldn't do it alone. I needed someone who could help me deal with such blatant hatred and, of course, with the media.

Obviously, every station wanted to interview me, but only to humiliate me more, not to listen to what I had to say. Everyone wanted a piece of me to hold up like a trophy: "Here's the one they banished!"

That's why we decided to give just one single interview. An interview of our choosing, where I knew I would feel respected. We would not have a list of conditions. Everything was fair game, but we demanded respect and the freedom to say whatever we had to say. By that point, all the media outlets were completely on the side of my mother, even though she was still maintaining her silence. No journalist wanted to offend her. They needed her exclusives to keep their ratings high and she knew that as well.

Iris and I chose Telemundo, because of the good relationship I had with Mun2, and Azucena Cierco, because she had always been gentle and polite with my family.

The interview was scheduled for the last week of October. It would be conducted in Los Angeles. It was terrifying to think about how my mother might react, but on the other hand, my hope was that if she saw me on TV, her heart would soften a bit and she would give me the chance to speak with her in private. It was my way of crying out to her, of begging her, "Please, Momma, listen to me."

We arrived at the hotel and Telemundo already had everything set up. Azucena and I prayed together before we began, and I told her, "I'm going to say whatever my heart dictates." There was no script, no prepared questions.

My family was really upset. I didn't warn them about the interview, so it came as a total surprise, like a bucket of ice water being dumped on them. But at that point, I didn't care. They'd officially turned their backs on me for a long time. What else did I have to lose?

In fact, I found out that they had a meeting with my mother where they all listened to her reasons, and they thought that it was only fair that I be given the same chance. Well, it never happened. I was denied my chance to attend that family meeting.

What this interview will do, then, is give them a chance to hear my words, I thought, without hesitation.

The only ones willing to give me a chance to defend myself were my grandma and grandpa. And, of course, my tío Juan.

When I sat in that chair opposite Azucena, all I could think about were my siblings, especially Johnny. They'd told me that my mother spoke about the problem in front of them, down to the gory details, and that Johnny now hated Esteban violently. My baby must have been so confused. Until two weeks ago, Esteban had been his hero! Would he hate me too now? So much stress, my God!

"And rolling!" ordered the producer standing next to the camera. Azucena was very cautious with my emotions and she let me speak freely. In my mind, it was all very clear as to whom I was really addressing: my mother, my aunts and uncles, but most of all, my babies. *These words go out to you, because I miss all of you so much*, I thought. *Listen to what they won't let me tell you in person: that I did not do these terrible things.*

In my head, the half hour passed quickly. That's it. I did it. Through that lens, I had faced the world, the Rivera family and my mother. I told them that I had never slept with Esteban, and that I didn't understand where such an accusation could have come from. I told them that my mother and I were going through a rough patch, but that everything would be resolved soon enough, whenever we were able to finally talk face-to-face. I asked my mother to give me that opportunity to talk in person. I told her I loved her and that I always would. And I thanked Azucena and Iris for giving me the courage to be there and say what I felt. But deep down I doubted that my words would have their desired effect. Would my mother listen? Would she listen with her heart or with her anger?

Indeed, the reaction was swift, and my mother damned me to hell in front of the entire planet with a devastating Tweet: *Your tears, your lies do not move me . . . You know, I know, and God knows the truth. Good luck.*

Good luck, Chiquis, I thought after reading it. I had now been publically condemned. Until then, the accusations were mere tabloid gossip, but now that Tweet had validated them. The entire world just read that Jenni had officially condemned her daughter, so therefore the rumors about Chiquis and Esteban must be true.

From Twitter to YouTube, the relentless Internet had it in for me.

It was the night of the Radio Awards. How could I forget the encounter between my boyfriend and my mother, especially since it was captured by dozens of camera phones!

The video clearly shows him insulting my mother and her friend Vanessa. "Step aside, let those filthy pigs through," he said loud enough for everyone to hear. Obviously, he was drunk. Drunk and hurt by all the sadness and suffering he saw me dealing with each and every night. Unlike the rest of my family, he bore witness to my agony.

Before getting into her car, my mother challenged him to show some respect and to sit down and talk in private. She defended herself and she did it well.

My mother didn't deserve that insult, regardless of what we were suffering from or enduring in private. And my boyfriend stopped and lowered his head. He knew full well not to argue or press the issue any further. Many interpreted that as a sign of weakness, but he told me later that he knew instantly that he'd messed up bad, and that he didn't want to make matters any worse. Better to keep quiet and accept your mistake.

Was he right to do what he did? Of course not! A man always has to respect a woman, especially when it's his girlfriend's mother. And I told him that later the same night, when we talked after the incident. I made it abundantly clear that no matter what was going on between my mother and me, he had to respect her. He promised he would and even tried to call her a few days later to apologize, though without success. My mother wouldn't take his calls. But despite the whole mess, I can't deny that I appreciated having someone stand up for me publicly. It was rude, yes, but I know my boyfriend was just trying to defend me. Maybe the way he did it wasn't in the best taste, but finally someone had dared to stand up to the Diva.

And my mother, instead of dismissing this unpleasant episode, returned to Twitter to air the dirty laundry. She challenged him, writing:

It's good that you believe her version and you want to defend your "girlfriend" . . . but that's not how things are done. Face me the right way, not like you're showing off your bravery. Talk the way civilized people talk. That way you won't spark huge scandals like this. Make an appointment with me. Lastly, as you see, I'm not afraid and I'll face any man like you. @chiquis626, congrats on your boyfriend. Good job.

So yeah, she publicly offered to set up an appointment to talk and listen to my boyfriend in private, yet she changed her number and there was no way to get ahold of her. And she wouldn't accept a single e-mail from me. Right away, I responded through the only means that I had left: damn Twitter.

Mother @jennirivera, exactly my point . . . You're telling him to talk to you the way civilized people talk . . . just like ME, your DAUGHTER, has the right to be heard. I haven't talked with you for about a month because you won't give me the time of day. But, like I said, you should take the time to listen. After all, I deserve it. I love you.

And Esteban? Where was he during this war of insults and tweets? Because there was a price on his head as well.

The truth is, I didn't know anything about him. Even the idea of contacting him still scared me. Iris called him to make sure he was safe and sound. Eventually, I decided it would be best if we each waged our own battles. If we were to be photographed together—even if we were simply trying to clarify the truth or lend support to one another—it would only be seen as confirmation that we were in a relationship, and nothing could have been further from the truth. And giving a joint interview would only add to the morbid curiosity and everyone would be more focused on how we acted together or how we looked at one another than they would be on what we had to say.

The strange machinations of public relations: when good people have to stop talking to each other in order to prove their innocence.

Forgive me, Esteban, if I didn't do the right thing. This is a book about forgiveness, and I'm also asking him to forgive me, as I will forgive him if he wasn't sure where to place his chips during those months and in more recent times. Forgive and be forgiven. Let it be so! The game of life—especially when played under the microscope of fame—can be a very complicated one indeed.

Days went by and November arrived. And then one morning, crying over my tea, I said to myself, *Enough already!* I remembered an expression in English that always seemed to lift my spirits: "It can only get better." When you're down, the only way to go is up. I decided up was the way I wanted to go and I decided to go to therapy. Not even the love of my friends and my boyfriend was enough to free me on its own.

I hadn't been to see a therapist since what happened with my father. This time, the reason for my visit was my mother. How ironic is that?

During our third session, the therapist told me, "Chiquis, perhaps it's time to start to visualize life without your mother. You need to start living your life the way it is now, not the way it was in the past."

Those words flowed deep into my soul. This was my life now, in November of 2012: Chiquis without her mother, without her siblings, without her aunts and uncles, but with her friends and boyfriend. With her salon and her business ventures. That was my reality, and I was going to run with it.

"This is my life now and I have to get over my mother," I remember saying to Dayanna. "It's like when a boyfriend leaves you for someone else. And this love of my life just left me."

"She might have left you, but you're not alone, sister," Dayanna said comfortingly. "There are many hearts out there who are asking about you, even if they don't know you personally."

And she was right. Right off the bat, Beto Cuevas, the popular Chilean artist, was one of those beautiful souls who had the balls to intervene on my behalf, despite not even knowing me. We'd never met and hadn't even spoken, but some mutual friends told me that during the recording of *La Voz . . . Mexico*—where both he and my mother were judges—he gently yet firmly rebuked her: "I don't care what happened between you and your daughter. You have to talk to her." My mother adored Beto, and they were great colleagues, but she never took his advice. Thank you, Beto, for trying. I send you my gratitude through these lines. Your reputation for being a good human being precedes you. And thank you, also, for being a good friend to my mother. Good friends, like you, sow peace, not war.

With the support of my friends and those kind souls who prayed for me, I woke up on Thanksgiving Day, one of the biggest days of the year for the Rivera family. It was our most celebrated holiday of the year, one that nobody wanted to miss, and that I had always been in charge of organizing. Needless to say, I wasn't invited to any of the family gatherings. My tío Juan tried to host one of them at his home in order to include me, but had no luck. Everybody went to Tío Pete's house, and again, needless to say, I wasn't welcome there either.

That silent Thursday morning, I lit a candle and said my prayers, and after reading my devotional, I felt in my heart that I should write one last e-mail to my mother.

This one would have a different tone. I now knew that my mother wasn't interested in hearing my arguments in my own defense, so I wasn't going to bother her with any more of that. This time, my intent would be to send peace, love and gratitude. In this message, I wanted simply to apologize if I had ever offended her with either my actions or my words. I asked her to forgive me for not understanding what was going on in her heart and in her mind, and that I was only then coming to understand that this might be another one of life's lessons that she was teaching me. And finally, that I accepted it with complete and utter humility.

On that peaceful morning, I thought and meditated. Maybe all this was a sign. Maybe I needed to show what I was made of, to stop being the daughter behind La Diva, to grow some thicker skin. *Okay, Momma, if that's why you're doing this, then you've succeeded. And if I can survive this, there's nothing in this life that can break me.*

Sometimes you have to be cruel in order to be kind. In this final e-mail to my mother, I humbly accepted that proverb and its consequences. I accepted whatever reason or lesson there might be behind my penance.

I ended my e-mail with *I love you, Momma* and I sent it to my tía Rosie, begging her to send it to my mother. She agreed to do so and asked that I wait a few hours.

And so I wouldn't be waiting alone, staring at my computer screen, I ended up accepting an invitation to Thanksgiving dinner at my friend Briana's house in Whittier. Her mom, Delia Hauser, welcomed me into her home, and showered me with hugs and affection. For the first time in two months, I felt the warmth of a real family. For a couple of hours, I allowed myself to dream that everything would be okay and that I wouldn't miss being surrounded by so much love. I am eternally grateful for that night, for the Hauser family taking me in like one of their own. I love you all.

After dinner, I returned alone to my apartment. I took one last look at my e-mails. There was nothing. An empty inbox. No response to my words of peace and love.

All that came was a text from Tía Rosie, who swore that my mother read the message, and that tears began to flow when she was done. That Jenni herself asked the whole family for just a few more days, that soon enough she would fix everything, and that we all just had to be patient.

I didn't know what to think. I was tired of waiting. That was the only thing Rosie ever said—wait, just wait—and now it was my mother who was asking for a little more time. Could it be that something was beginning to change in her heart? Exhausted from so much promise, I turned off my light, turned off all hope and went to sleep.

19.

WHEN A BUTTERFLY FLIES AWAY

Beep beep beep . . . Back in those days, that little sound of messages on my phone was so traumatizing that I didn't even want to check them. It was seven in the morning and I was lying there alone in a massive bed in a Las Vegas hotel, happy and exhausted from the night before. That weekend, my dear friend—my favorite cousin—Karina had gotten married, and I wouldn't have missed it for the world.

I took the opportunity to attend the event with my inseparable companions Gerald and Briana, and to celebrate my new life with them, giving thanks for everything I still had left: my health, my job, a few of my cousins, my boyfriend and my best friends.

Beep beep . . . Again with those damn messages. I tossed my phone away and rolled over.

Still half asleep between the sheets, I remembered the drive across the desert on I-15 the previous day. I'd had a premonition and I shared it with Briana and Gerald:

"You know what? Today I really miss my mother. I used to go

days without feeling like this. But the funny thing is that I get the feeling that she misses me too. Don't ask me how, but I know."

"You think she'll call you before Christmas comes?" Briana asked me.

"I don't know. Maybe, but I'm not holding out much hope. Not anymore. I feel like her anger has passed, but now she's not quite sure how to find her way back. I know her. Maybe now she realizes that it was all just a misunderstanding. I don't know, boo, I just don't know, but for the first time in a while, I get the feeling that she wants to speak with me."

"I hope that's the case," Gerald said, encouragingly. "But in the meantime, remember the promise: we're going to Vegas to begin a new stage—Chiquis Time!"

"Chiquis Time, here we come!" I shouted with relief. And I stepped on the gas.

As soon as we got to the hotel where we'd all be staying, my tío Gus and the rest of my cousins welcomed me warmly. It seemed as if the drama was starting to calm down, at least among some members of the Rivera family. My mother wouldn't be attending because she had to give a performance in Monterrey, Mexico, that same night, which meant they wouldn't be forced to choose who to invite: her or me. I'd finally be able to see my brothers and sisters for the first time in ages. I missed them so much! Though I wasn't quite sure how they would react to seeing me.

The wedding was celebrated on Saturday afternoon at the legendary Little White Chapel. It was very romantic, and I finally got to see my beloved cousin marry her high school sweetheart, Eddie.

After the ceremony I could finally see the kids again, who were all there with Jacqie. "Hey, sister," is all I got from her. She didn't even touch me. Total cold shoulder. Her movements and the look in her eye were exactly like those of my mother. Jacqie has always been her spitting image and that remains true to this day.

Jenicka was the only one who dared to give me a hug, but even that felt tense. Her nervous eyes didn't seem to want to make contact with mine.

But the one that finally killed me was the reaction by my little Johnny. He refused to kiss me, spun around and ran to hide behind Jacqie.

Choking back my tears, I prayed to God for him. It's so unfair when children get dragged into problems between adults and leave them so confused. I'd been told that he even ripped the head off of the figurine he had of Esteban, which was part of the collection my stepfather had given him. Why did they have to fill that poor little boy's head with grown-up garbage? That's what really hurt me.

Since the banquet ended early, I decided to continue the party over at the VooDoo Rooftop Nightclub at the Rio Hotel with Briana and Gerald. Just the three of us. It was Saturday night in Vegas, time to reinvent myself and unleash the fun. It was high time to put an end to two months of being holed up in my apartment.

The music the DJ was spinning, and the terrace and the spectacular view of the city that never sleeps moved me deeply. While I was dancing in the crowd, I looked up at the sky, and all of a sudden I felt a sharp pain in my heart, and I was overcome by a profound sense of sadness from head to toe. It was something physical. I could feel it in my arms and legs. I looked at the time: one in the morning.

"What's up?" Gerald shouted over the music.

"Nothing. Just tired," I lied. "I think I'm gonna sit down. You two keep dancing."

I left the dance floor and headed back to our table. Without knowing why, I burst into tears.

"What's wrong, boo?" Briana asked, not knowing what was going on.

"I don't know. I want to go. Let's head back to the room."

"But we just got here," Gerald protested.

"Sorry, guys. I guess I'm just not feeling too good," I said. I didn't want to explain that, once again, I was thinking about my mother. They'd call me out for being a drag.

When we got back to the room, we ordered some McDonald's, we talked, we laughed and that strange bout of sadness gradually faded away. Still, though, I kept waking up every hour or so throughout the night and on into the dawn of Sunday, December 9. Tossing and turning. I just couldn't sleep. And to make matters worse, those *beep beep*s had been buzzing from my phone, which was now at the foot of the bed, since the earliest hours of the morning.

Around ten o'clock I got the fateful call that got me out of bed and explained why I'd been getting all those messages.

"Hey, cousin, it's Karina. Are you still in Las Vegas?"

"Yes, we're here. Totally racked out. Why?"

"My dad's already back in Long Beach, and he called me. We have to get back there right away."

"Why? I don't understand."

"I don't know, cousin. He said check Twitter."

"Okay, got it," I said, and hung up.

And that's when I saw it:

Plane carrying Jenni Rivera disappears midflight. No traces of the five passengers or two crewmembers. A search for the private jet continues. It is feared that there were no survivors. The plane lost contact with the tower ten minutes after takeoff, at exactly 3:10 a.m.

My first reaction was, *What bullshit! More bad reporting about my mother by the media. I'm sure she's fine and this is all just pure speculation.* God forgive me for not believing it at first, but it was just too incredible and too painful to process. Besides, in this day and age, it's all too common to hear through social media that so-and-so died, but then it turns out to be a complete fabrication. But all of a sudden, I remembered the fit of sadness that came over me the previous night, right in the middle of the dance floor. It was one o'clock in Vegas, which meant it was three in Monterrey. It was a bad omen.

I called Tía Rosie.

"Don't worry, Chiquis, we're trying to get some clarification," she said, quite calmly. "It's still too early to say anything."

Next I called my tío Juan. If anyone was going to tell me the truth, it would be him.

"I hope the reports aren't true. I'm sure she's safe and sound somewhere. Maybe they just got held up." He was worried, and searching for answers.

"No one's been able to get in touch with her?"

"She's not answering her phone. Nobody is."

"Nobody? Who else was on that plane?" My heart stopped.

"Jacob and Arturo, that we know of. They're not answering their phones either. Sounds like they're turned off."

My heart sank. Jacob Yebale, my mother's official makeup artist, was more than an employee. He was our friend, confidante and a veteran of our battles. Losing him would be like losing a member of the family.

"The best thing would be to head straight to Grandma's house," Tío Juan recommended. "We're all going over there."

Fifteen minutes later, we were loading up my car. Briana was silent. She could see the fear in my eyes. Gerald was trying to be encouraging, but it didn't work.

Once again we drove across the Mojave Desert. But this time, it felt endless, frigid, horrible and empty.

I asked to be the one behind the wheel. I wanted to feel like I was in control of the situation, to keep busy and not let my mind wander. No thoughts, good or bad. I didn't want to talk about it. I begged my friends not to comment on anything. I didn't even want to listen to music, until I finally got tired of staring down the straight line of the highway, and I turned on the radio. K-LOVE 107.5 FM was on the dial. They were playing my mother's songs, and the commentators were reporting on the search in great detail: "They have found clothing and the remains of an aircraft. Still no confirmation on whether the remains are those of Jenni Rivera."

That was when it really hit me hard. The fear had become a reality.

"If it's on the radio, then it's true!" I started to shout. "God wouldn't do something like this to me! I still haven't spoken to her! We haven't fixed things yet!"

I was going crazy and shouting the same things over and over again, but I didn't want to pull over and hand the wheel over to someone else. Briana and Gerald kept quiet and hid their fears that I'd wreck the car. There was no way I was getting out of the driver's seat, and there were no words that could have calmed me down.

"God, You can't do this to me!" I was screaming like a mental patient. "It's not true! No, no, no!"

My poor, dear friends. I ask your forgiveness for putting you in such a dangerous situation there on the highway. My head was spinning to the point where it was about to come unhinged and all I wanted to do was get to Lakewood and learn that it was all just a horrible misunderstanding. Because at the end of the day, we Riveras are experts when it comes to misunderstanding things.

"We will always remember *La Diva de la Banda*, with that beautiful smile of hers," the commentator said. And I stepped on the gas.

We made it from Las Vegas to Lakewood in three hours flat. God didn't want anything to happen to us. There, outside the house, a scene of utter chaos was waiting for us. Reporters, photographers, fans and onlookers. Everyone was yelling and trying to talk to me at the same time. I fought my way out of the car and ran to the front door, with Briana and Gerald by my side.

Inside of my grandma's house, a horrible silence reigned. The entire family was already there, but nobody said a word. All you could hear was the distant murmur of the crowd outside.

Should I even be here? I thought, racked with guilt. *If everyone really thinks I slept with my mother's husband, should I be here, crying with them?* Gerald and Briana saw the fear on my face and decided to stay with me, taking turns standing beside me and holding my hand. I was so grateful to them! They gave me the strength to be there, at least until someone broke the ice in that room full of fear.

It was my tía Rosie who took the initiative and said to me, "Chiquis, stay here. We have to stick together. Now more than ever." Mikey ran up to hug me, and Jacqie—who so far had only been watching me from a corner of the room—put her doubts aside and wrapped her arms around me.

"Chiquis," she said tearfully, "the kids need you. We all do."

Finally sure that this was where I belonged, and feeling welcome, I sat down with the children, who immediately latched on to me out of desperation. Johnny hugged me with all his might, and gone was all the hatred and resentment and all the things people said about me. He laid his head down on my lap and began to cry softly. My baby couldn't lose both of his mothers in this world. Jenicka couldn't either.

∽

For the next few hours, I listened only to the information that came through my tío Juan and my tía Rosie. The two of them were on the phone, along with my tío Lupe in Mexico, managing the situation and speaking with the authorities.

"Don't worry. We're going to find her," Juan said. More than anyone, he was refusing to accept the facts we were getting. "I'm contacting some people who know some people there in Mexico. People who might know whether she's been kidnapped."

Thinking about ransom notes instead of plane crashes gave him strength. The same with my grandpa Pedro.

By midafternoon, we had confirmation that the wreckage found in the foothills outside Iturbide, Nuevo León, was in fact from my mother's plane. There were no survivors.

Nobody left the house there in Lakewood. We spent the night there in vigil, collapsed in the living room or pacing around the kitchen.

At some point, late in the night, my dear Jenicka said to me, "Sister, I don't know what happened between you and Mom, but it doesn't matter to me anymore. We need you."

"And I need you all even more," I replied with the biggest hug in the world. "Don't worry, I won't leave you guys alone for a moment."

Eventually, I fell asleep on the couch with Johnny in my arms. My baby was crying even in his sleep, and he asked me, "Why did this happen to my mom? Why?" I didn't let go of him for three straight days.

Around noon on Monday, my tío Lupe arrived straight from Monterrey, where the authorities had confirmed more details about the accident.

He and his manager came inside the Lakewood house and collapsed on the couch insensitively.

"No way anybody survived that. *Nadie*. Believe me," he informed us all.

"But what are we doing, all standing around here? Why aren't there any family members there?" I shouted at my tío Juan. "I heard that Arturo and Jacob's families are already on their way." Until that moment, I'd remained silent, but now was the time for me to resume my position as Jenni's oldest daughter.

"Chiquis, there's nothing we can do there. Why go?" Tío Lupe insisted.

"We have to go! Don't you hear me? Someone needs to go bring me back my mother! I want her here, one way or another! Bring her home! Just bring her to me!" I said.

My sadness was turning into anger. But I felt so powerless. I couldn't just hop on a plane and leave the children there alone, but on the other hand I was desperate to go climb up that damn mountain, find my mom and carry her home in my own arms, if needed.

In the end, Lupe agreed to go back, and a coin flip would decide who went with him. Between Gustavo and Juan, it fell to Gus.

"Forget the coin toss. All three of you are going," I said, looking them all straight in the eye. "Tío Juan, you too."

Having Tío Juan there meant we would be informed about even the smallest detail. He would be my eyes on the ground there in Monterrey.

That Monday afternoon, my mind was telling me, *That accident is real. Nobody could walk out of those hills alive.* But my heart kept repeating, *Maybe she was kidnapped before she got on that plane, and she's being held somewhere alive.* My mind feverish with pain, I even came to believe that she could have bailed out before the crash, and that now she was lying there, hurt, somewhere in those mountains. Any story would be better than the one we were seeing unfold on television. It's so much easier to accept the truth when it doesn't hurt so much! So much easier for others to resign themselves to having lost her, when for me it meant never having a chance to reconcile!

"Stay calm, Chiquis," my tía Rosie said. "When your mom comes home, you're gonna be the first one she hugs when she walks through that door. Maybe all this is a sign that our family needs to come together. Maybe it's a divine lesson."

But when Tuesday came, I knew there would be no embrace, no reconciliation. That morning, while following the news online, I stumbled upon a few photos, which many people have since wondered if I saw. Yes. Unfortunately I did. They showed the remains of a woman's foot there in the accident site, and the remains of long, blond hair.

The hair could have belonged to anyone, but I know my mother's feet. I even put her shoes on for her, whenever she was tired or getting ready for a big event.

"Jenicka," I asked, "What color nail polish was Mom wearing?"

"Red. Why?" she asked, innocently.

"No reason, baby. Just wondering."

I ran into the bathroom so the children wouldn't hear me, and I collapsed, bawling, on the ground, surrounded by the flowery towels and the thousands of powerfully scented soaps that my grandma Rosa always likes to buy. Suddenly, my tears subsided, and I felt my mother speaking to me: "Get ready, Chiquis." I could hear her voice in my head just as clearly as if she were standing in front of me. "I'm not coming home, and you're going to have to take care of my babies from now on. Make sure they're ready to hear the news. They're in good hands with you. Be brave, Chiquis." Right there, I closed my eyes and I prayed. I prayed for her soul and I swore that I would always take care of my siblings. I had a long conversation with her, but only about the children. I was certain that she heard me. Finally, my mom was giving me the chance to speak with her, even if it was soul to soul instead of face-to-face. I told her one more time how much I loved her. "I love you, my princess," she said, and that was good-bye.

I opened my eyes and went back out into the living room. Johnny was looking at me from the couch.

"Listen, you have to be strong, *papas*. There's a ninety-five percent chance that Mom isn't going to come home alive."

He didn't answer. There just weren't any words. I sat down next to him and we embraced in tears. We cried inconsolably for nearly an hour. *God, dear God, why did you take his dad away from him, and now do the same with his mom? My poor baby.* I swear, at that moment I was crying more for his loss than for my own. To this day, I feel that the ones who lost the most were my Jenicka and my Johnny.

That night, I locked myself in the bathroom clutching a picture of my mother, and I told her, "Help me. I need help. Tell me how to console the kids. Tell me what I have to do. I'm scared!"

Nothing. I didn't hear her voice this time. Just total silence.

When dawn came, I would have to summon up all my courage and get the ship afloat. Those were two long agonizing weeks before my mother's body would be returned to us, when we could bid farewell to her the way she deserved. Dayanna stayed with me for those two weeks. At nights, after the kids fell asleep, I would turn to Dayanna and say to her, crying, "Sister, I don't know what I'm going to do." I felt confused and scared.

When it came to those grisly photos of the accident that were circulating all over the Internet, I tried my best to keep the kids from seeing them, but that proved to be impossible. Johnny came across them on his iPad, and showed them to my grandma. And now I'd like to address the people who published them: What if it were your mother? How would you feel if one day the entire world could see your mother the way we had to see ours?

There are those mindless individuals out there who—it can only be said—have no mothers, and never will.

Another petty act that hurt the soul during those nights of waiting and mourning was the news that the crash site was looted, either before or during the arrival of rescuers and investigators. I wasn't worried about the jewelry, even though my mother would have been wearing some of her most valuable pieces on this flight. I wasn't concerned with her expensive bags or shoes that were so unscrupulously removed from the location. I didn't even care about the hundreds of thousands of dollars in cash that were supposedly paid to my mother hours before for the concert in Monterrey. If she was carrying that money with her and it was stolen from the crash site, so be it!

What hurt the most was her BlackBerry. The person who took that has no idea how much pain that caused me. People carry their lives and their thoughts with them on their phones. My mother noted of all her ideas, plans and words on that BlackBerry. And some of those words were, more than likely, for me. That phone may very well have contained the key to alleviating my pain, the answers to so many questions. That little gadget contained her final message and her final joke. Who was it for?

Half an hour before the flight was to take off, my mother changed her profile picture on her BlackBerry messenger, and put one up of her brothers and sister. Could it be true that she really was hoping to make peace and bring everyone back together soon?

Farewell to that phone, if it managed to survive the impact intact.

We spent days dialing her number in the wild hopes that someone would answer and tell us that it had all been a horrible nightmare. But all we ever heard was her greeting: "Hi, this is Jenni, please leave a message" until her voice mail box was full, and our hearts were left empty.

20.
GRADUATING WITH HONORS

Chiquis, look at this picture of your mom at the concert in Monterrey. The stage was in the shape of a cross. It was a premonition!" a friend said to me once.

"Look at this interview your mom gave before the concert. She says she already achieved everything she wanted, and that she was grateful and satisfied with her life. Your mom knew it was her final night. She was saying good-bye," repeated a journalist on the phone.

While we were waiting for more news out of Mexico, there was a constant barrage of gossip and rumors. Once again, here came the toxic voices looking to poison us in the hopes of earning our attention.

Honestly, for me, it was all just coincidence. People who were actually with her that night have told me that she—when she saw the cross-shaped stage—was simply happy, and saw nothing ominous in it: "I love it! It's beautiful!" she said excitedly.

In my heart, more than a premonition, that stage and those final words were a message of peace that she is in heaven. A message of reassurance.

Any other speculation or stories about the great beyond are, to me, pure bullshit.

As for the song she chose to perform that night—"Paloma Negra" ("Black Dove")—that did have a hidden message. For once, the speculation was right, although the message wasn't anything supernatural.

It was the same song she had dedicated to Jacqie two years earlier, when she left home after a stupid fight, and my mother was asking her to come back.

That same song, now dedicated to me, on that beautiful stage, was without a doubt her way of saying to me, "It's time for you to come home as well, princess."

Through "Paloma Negra," my mother was very clearly saying to me, "I miss you. I don't know how to fix all this. I don't know how to work my way back."

Black dove, black dove, where oh where will you go . . .

My mother wasn't saying good-bye to me or to anyone else with those lyrics. She was searching for the path to forgiveness. And that's not just in my imagination. For days, my tía Rosie had been insinuating that everything would change come Christmastime, and nobody knew my mother's plans better than her beloved sister.

God grant me the strength, for I'm dying to go and find her.

To this day, I can't listen to the recording of that concert in Monterrey. It still hurts too much.

"Okay, what are we going to say when they ask us what's going on with Chiquis?" Tío Juan was the one who dared to ask the obvious question, while everyone else was rushing to prepare for the big ceremony in my mother's honor.

Nobody knew what to say. My tía Rosie had told everyone that my mother had read my letter on Thanksgiving Day and that she had been planning to reconcile. And everyone agreed that it would be unfair for the world to continue to condemn me for the rest of my life for something that was left unclear and only half understood at best.

I think it was a combination of instinct and love that whenever the media would ask about me, the family would say, "Chiquis is fine; she's with the rest of the family. Yes, yes, she was able to speak with her mother before the accident. They patched everything up."

It was a beautiful attempt to protect me and shield me from the public eye. This was no time to be dealing with outrage from the fans. But for me, it just wasn't enough. I kept insisting that to say my mother forgave me is to accept that I committed the crime, and I didn't do anything wrong! I was looking for complete and total absolution, not just forgiveness. My grandma Rosa, as always, made me see reason: "Chiquis, now is not the time to argue. Look at what we're dealing with here," she begged.

Okay, for the time being, I accepted those good intentions. Right now, the priority was calming our pain.

And something that both scared and hurt me was going back to the house in Encino. The children needed clean clothes and a few other things, because the ceremony had been delayed. The bureaucracy involved in recovering my mother's body was really dragging things out. It was all going so slowly. Dayanna accompanied me along with Johnny and Jenicka. The four of us drove to Encino for the first time since the incident. It was raining really hard that day and we all had lumps in our throats, not knowing what to say.

The tears started rolling down our cheeks as soon as we opened the front door. The mansion felt empty and cold. Nobody was laughing in the kitchen, nobody was singing in the living room, no one was shouting on the phone in the office. And my mother was watching us from the framed photographs that stood on the piano and hung from the walls.

In her bedroom, her bed was just as she had left it five days before: her pajamas off to one side, the sheets rumpled up and a book lying on the blanket. I threw myself on top of the pillows, and as I breathed in the scent of her perfume, I burst into tears.

It was the same bed where I would tell her all of my problems, and where she would console and advise me, all the while gently stroking my hair.

"God, this is not how I dreamed about returning to this house someday. No, not like this." I protested, crying to the Lord.

On a chair next to the nightstand I saw one of her red dresses that she must have worn before leaving for Monterrey. I grabbed it and put it in a plastic Ziploc bag that I found in the kitchen.

"I'll keep it forever," I said to Dayanna. "I don't want her scent to ever go away."

With pain in my heart, we left that bedroom so filled with memories and began to gather up the shoes and clothing that Jenicka and Johnny would need. We also put a few pictures of my mother in a bag, and with that, we left. The emotions were too intense for us to stay there even a minute longer.

"Have you heard from Esteban, sister?" Dayanna asked as we rolled down the hill.

Esteban had called me the day of the accident. It was the first time we'd spoken directly since the whole mess began. We didn't talk at all about the scandal. All our attention and all of our words were focused on my mother and the accident. He sounded so sad!

I swear that Esteban still loved her, despite the fact that she had walked out of his life and publically humiliated him.

"Chiquis, I want to be there with you and the kids. I want to be there for you during all this," he begged. I told him he should ask the rest of the family, because I was in no position to be making such decisions. Tío Juan and Grandma Rosa said yes, but Tía Rosie was against the idea.

Interestingly enough, the rest of my aunts and uncles bore him no ill will. Not even secretly. Like me, they all believed Esteban was a good husband and a good stepfather. That's the only thing we saw. If he had been unfaithful, or anything else like that, none of us had ever seen it. God only knows, or perhaps my mother did, but she never showed us any concrete evidence.

But with everything that had happened recently, my tía Rosie was afraid that if we allowed him into the house in Lakewood, it would only generate more unwanted rumors. Esteban wouldn't give up, though. He called me the night before the ceremony— which would be broadcast internationally on a number of different channels—and again he pleaded: he wanted to be there.

"No, Chiquis," my aunt refused once again. "With so many cameras there, his presence would just be a distraction. Remember, the true purpose here is to honor your mother, to dedicate each and every moment to her."

This time, my tía Rosie was quite right. Public relations and what people might say left Esteban excluded. Therefore, again, I ask for your forgiveness, Esteban, for not including your pain with that of the family.

The Celestial Graduation of Jenni Rivera took place on Wednesday, December 19. By then, they had recovered my mother. I won't say "her remains," as it was said in the media. I prefer to say "my mother."

We also refused to call it a funeral or a memorial. Dolores Janney Rivera was always the best student. And one of her greatest dreams, which life wouldn't allow her to achieve, was to graduate from a great university. Her three oldest children were also unable to give her that joy. So on that day, we decided to fulfill that dream. Now, we would see her graduate with the highest degree that can be earned in this world: the final diploma granted to us by God. Jenni Rivera would graduate from this life with honors.

That Wednesday, our favorite day of the week, we left the house in Lakewood at four in the morning to avoid the media and get to the Gibson Amphitheatre early. We left our cars in a nearby parking lot and got in an RV that would take us around the back, near the stage entrance. We had donuts, and we fixed our hair and made ourselves up for the big moment.

My poor Jacob! He, who had done our makeup on the most important days of our lives, was not there on that December morning to make us laugh and make us shine beautifully inside and out. The whole family will always remember those who were with my mother on that plane: from our dear Jacob, to Arturo Rivera, my mother's friend and publicist, who helped turn her into a star in Mexico, to Jorge Sánchez, the stylist who pampered her like a goddess, to Mario Macías, her faithful attorney who handled a thousand and one tasks. That morning, while we waited, we prayed not only for my mother, but for all of them. We will never forget them, nor will we forget the pilots, Mr. Miguel Pérez and his young co-pilot, Alessandro Torres. We privately mourned them all, because they were my mother's final companions, and they will forever be a part of our mourning.

After the final prayer had been uttered, it was time to walk out onto that tremendous stage. The Gibson was where my mother had grown to become a star in front of her adoring Los Angeles fans, her homies. And it was there that we all would bid farewell to her cocoon, her cocoon made from the finest wood, where our beautiful butterfly lay at rest. We refused to refer to it in any other way.

When the music began, I took a deep breath, squeezed Johnny and Jenicka's hands tightly, and together we took our first few steps toward that beautiful cocoon at the front of that enormous stage, joining the rest of our family.

Immediately, the most tender and passionate applause I have ever heard in my life filled us with warmth and love. I couldn't even cry. I was in something of a trance, like a zombie. As if there were a gentle drunkenness in my soul.

I won't deny that, during the ceremony, I experienced a bit of embarrassment and a few moments of intense anxiety. There were a number of great artists sitting in the front row who blindly believed that I had betrayed my mother. I didn't dare make eye contact with them. I could also make out Ferny among them and I couldn't manage to look him in the face either. Sorry, Ferny. My nerves got the best of me.

When it came my turn to stand before the microphone and give my speech, I had to pull out a little slip of paper. The stress and fatigue prevented me from memorizing what I had written down. Once again, my mind was going crazy. *Thousands of eyes are watching me*, I said to myself. *What are they thinking? That I'm a whore, a hypocrite? Some kind of slut?* Oh God, all I wanted to do was focus on my mother, on her love, on her beautiful graduation filled with butterflies and applause, but it was so hard to do.

Right there, standing in front of the microphone, I heard my mother's voice again, something that hadn't happened since the previous week at my grandma's house. "Be strong, Chiquis. Be strong, *mija*. Momma is here with you. Don't worry. But don't bitch out either. Don't back down." And just like that afternoon at the grand opening of my salon, when I had to face the cameras all by myself, I felt someone grab my hand. I don't know if it was just my imagination, or if it was Johnny who was still latched on to me, but that hand helped me face the arena packed with thousands of fans on their feet, deeply emotional. *What if someone shouts something rude?* I asked myself. I felt that hand again, and all my fears vanished. I spent the rest of the graduation ceremony with a sense of profound peace.

I'll never forget the beautiful songs that Joan Sebastian and Ana Gabriel performed in honor of my mother. There could have been no better homage. Nor will I ever forget the words of Pepe Garza: "Jenni was perfect because of her imperfections." I could understand that better than anyone. I loved my mother because I knew that beneath her mistakes was a unique and special human being, and that her love extended beyond the scope of this world.

Once the ceremony was over, the audience formed a long line leading up to her cocoon so that they could leave white roses for their Diva. I stepped aside to let them pass, when all of a sudden the women and girls began to call to me: "Chiquis, come, come over here," and "Chiquis, come on, we want to give you a hug."

It took me a second or two to realize that they were offering me their forgiveness. My heart was bursting with gratitude. Gratitude toward the thousands of fans who showed me their love instead of their hatred. They showed me their true greatness, and I humbly accepted the gift they gave me, which was just as generous as the roses they left for my mother.

And in that same instant, I forgave everyone for all the cruelties that had been written about me on Twitter, and for their having convicted me without knowing the full truth. He is forgiven. She is forgiven. I harbor no ill will toward anyone. And I hope they harbor none toward me. I love them all.

I want the world to know that Jenni's fans gathered that morning to honor her, not to dishonor her memory with bitter looks. That they presented themselves just as they are: the best of the best. I will always be proud of them, and indebted to them for the rest of my life. I love you, J-Unit!

A few days after that lovely graduation ceremony, I had a dream about my mother. This dream was so real that when I woke up, my mind was reluctant to leave its state of trance.

We were all at the house in Encino. My mother entered the room, sat down next to me and wrapped her arms around me. She laughed, she chatted with everyone, but she wouldn't leave my side. I don't remember what we talked about; just that her body was permanently stuck to mine, and that we were both overflowing with joy.

You can chalk it up to craziness, or to my mind playing tricks on me as it searches desperately for an end to the pain of a daughter disowned, but that dream was just as real as life itself. Every once in a while, the things you want or hope for end up coming true in mysterious ways.

21.

PIECES OF MY HEART

"Now, Chiquis, now, *mija*, we have to give her a proper burial." My grandma was the one who was most insistent. She couldn't bear the thought that six days after the great Celestial Graduation, my mother was still lying in a cold refrigerator inside her beautiful cocoon.

"Grandma, just give me two more days. I want to see the final results from Monterrey. We can't rush this."

It had already been two weeks since the terrible accident, and the fans and the media alike had only one question: When would the funeral be? While I, in my newly recovered role as the oldest child, took the baton and refused to bury her. "I want all of her," I told my aunts and uncles time and again. I wasn't about to lose any little bit of my mother, however unpleasant that may sound.

The authorities in Mexico warned us that a number of parts had yet to be identified, and that a second round of DNA tests was still pending. It sounds horrific, but I'm telling it like it was. It would be another week before the final exams were conducted on the multiple body parts of the passengers remaining at the morgue. The impact of the plane must have been like that of a wartime missile.

It was my tío Gus's job to open the boxes as they arrived and put my mother into her cocoon with his own two hands. He was the bravest, and the one who had to swallow the most bitter of pills. I am eternally grateful to him. If it weren't for Tío Gus, I never would have believed that our butterfly was actually in there.

And while Juan and Gus were in charge of the most difficult of preparations, my tío Lupe was in the studio, recording a song dedicated to my mother. This didn't sit very well with either Juan or Gus. They couldn't believe that during this time of pain, before my mother had even been buried, Lupe already had a song ready to mix and master, and was getting ready to relaunch his career.

In fact, to this day, that song that my tío Lupe was in such a rush to release still causes fights in our family.

∞

"Okay, Chiquis, I just got the last shipment from Monterrey. Now it is time," Tío Gus told me. "The waiting is killing us all."

"No, tío. We have to run our own DNA test here. I'd never be able to sleep knowing that any other victims might be in here," I begged, feeling that I was going crazy in my efforts to recover what, up until that point, had been the blood of my blood. "I wouldn't feel right if we were to have someone other than my mother in this cocoon. It just wouldn't be right!"

If there was something I inherited from my mother, it was her stubbornness, and this time I won. We postponed the private funeral, which had been planned for that Wednesday, December 26, without specifying the reasons.

Though this delay did provoke some morbid speculations by

gossip columnists and other members of the tabloid media: that the Rivera family had postponed the funeral to gain publicity— that we were holding off on the burial so we could take my mother's body back to Monterrey and hold another Celestial Graduation, after selling the broadcasting rights to Televisa for millions— yes, I heard all that nonsense, and I didn't know whether to laugh or cry.

Finally, after receiving the last bit of DNA analysis, everything had been confirmed, and we decided on a date of December 31. We wanted to say good-bye to my mother along with the year, so that every time we celebrated New Year's Eve, we would be celebrating her. That would also give us the opportunity to begin 2013 with new goals and new energy, if we had any left.

We spent Christmas Day in Encino: the whole family was together there, though we didn't exchange big gifts or throw a huge party. We just unwrapped the presents that my mother had already bought for my cousins and some of my aunts. She didn't have time to finish her list, but I didn't want the gifts she did buy to stay there, piled up in her closet. That night, when everyone had left, I slept on the sofa in the living room with Johnny and Jenicka. None of us were prepared to officially return to this enormous house so filled with memories.

Now, we would spend the year's end at the burial site. We chose All Souls Mortuary in our beloved Long Beach. It couldn't have been anywhere else. It's the city where she was born, cried, laughed, fell down and got back up a thousand times over. It's her city.

My desire was to have her cremated so that her heart would once again be in one piece, and we could bring her ashes home with us. But my mother had written that there would be no cremation, and that she wanted to be buried. I remember how she liked to joke around and tell us, "When I die, bury me upside down, so that the haters can keep on kissing my ass." Ah, our Jenni . . . She was unique!

We decided that this ceremony—unlike her graduation—would be a very small and intimate event. No stars, no friends, no cameras and no flowers. Just parents, siblings, children and our closest relatives.

Well, we did add one more name to the list: Esteban Loaiza. My tío Juan managed to convince Tía Rosie that, since there would be no cameras, we'd be safe.

To our surprise, Esteban turned down our invitation. He was really upset with us, feeling that he'd been excluded during those two weeks of mourning. Besides, December 31 was his birthday, and it must have seemed in very bad taste to have chosen such a date to say good-bye to the woman he still loved.

And he was so right. Which is why, again, Esteban, I ask for your forgiveness on behalf of our family. So many mistakes were made when we were blinded by grief.

It was with much of that grief, on that cold winter morning in front of my mother's cocoon, surrounded by only Rivera family members, that Tío Juan and Tío Lupe improvised two songs that truly came from the heart, since nobody had prepared anything formal to say. We all spoke a few words of farewell, or shared an anecdote or two as we saw fit, but that time there was no public and no applause. That moment was just between Jenni and us. No one else.

The mortuary allowed us to take turns picking up dirt from ground and placing it on top of the cocoon. But first, Tío Juan placed a bundle of handwritten letters inside that we had composed the night before, including messages of love, photographs and a ring that I gave her for her last birthday. It was a promise ring, with a precious emerald, that signified my commitment to always honoring her and being a better daughter.

And there we left my mother: covered by a blanket of flowers and butterflies. Now the one who feels incomplete is me, because I left an enormous piece of my heart there as well.

22.
DUST IN THE SOUL

Sister, I want to sleep in my own bed now," Jenicka said after spending the last several nights on the giant couches facing the fireplace in the living room.

The three of us were still there, side by side, because Johnny and Jenicka didn't want to be separated, even to go to sleep. Well, me too, but for other reasons. I was finding it really difficult to officially settle back into the house of the woman who ran me out of her life. Even though deep down in my heart, I knew that my mother no longer held any resentment against me, it still wasn't easy to climb those stairs and go into my empty room or her bedroom, still filled with so many bittersweet memories.

"Don't even think about it," Jenicka said, as if reading my mind. "You're staying right here. This is your house, Chiquis. It always has been. And you can't leave us alone."

Okay, that was clear. I'd move out of my apartment in Van Nuys and start my new life taking care of the kids and the house just like old times. Just that this time, my mother wouldn't be here, and there would be new tenants in her place: my tía Rosie and her family.

"You knew that, right? She also handed custody over to Rosie."
My tío Juan had warned me about that several days earlier, even
though I knew all the legal details of my mother's will, which was
read to us once it had been confirmed that she hadn't survived the
accident.

My mother named her sister Rosie as the executor of her estate,
but what really broke me was that she also named Rosie the guardian of Johnny and Jenicka. I couldn't believe my mother would be
so vindictive. We all went to the reading of the will, where I was
handed the amendment cutting me out. I was still in shock from
my mother's death, but what shocked me most was that everyone
told me that they didn't agree with my mother's decision, but nobody stood up for me or suggested that it be corrected. Not my
uncles, not my tía Rosie. Nobody.

My mother had always been a great businesswoman, very organized and very prudent. As such, a few months earlier, she'd formed
a trust so that she could be sure that her children would benefit
directly and for their entire lives from everything she had worked
so hard to earn. My mother always said that all her hard work and
all her sacrifices were for her children. My grandma and grandpa
weren't even included in the will for this reason. However, my tía
Rosie was also put in charge of the administration of this trust for
life.

I can't deny the fact that being left out of my mother's last will
made me feel even more awkward about being in that house. What
was I, then? A guest? Someone on the lease? A roommate?

"Who cares what's in those papers?" Johnny said. "In this
house, you're Chiquis."

Yes! I didn't need to have my name listed in some document
to be with my babies, so I resigned myself to a life of uncertainty
in exchange for the chance to be with them. Tía Rosie was busy

enough with her own husband and daughter, besides being pregnant again, so from day one I put myself in charge of the kids, just as I had been since the day they were born. Only now, I would have to ask my aunt for permission for many things.

It was strange, and I have to say it did create some tension. I had to consult with her on everything, from school to groceries to the daily expenses of running a household, which was new for her as well, since she had never lived with us before. The simple task of taking the kids to the doctor became incredibly complicated.

One night Jenicka was having a very severe panic attack, but when we got to the hospital, they told me, "I'm sorry, but we're going to need her guardian to sign off on this." I had to get Tía Rosie out of bed in the middle of the night, and I felt next to useless.

But that didn't matter. The children were well worth hassles like this, and many more.

And my mother's will and custody issues were not the only legal issues we had to face. With the accident came more lawyers, lawsuits, investigations and bureaucracy than we ever thought imaginable. Saying good-bye to Jenni Rivera had kicked up a riot!

The private Learjet, which took off from Monterrey en route to Toluca, crashed on December 9 between 3:10 and 3:20 a.m. near Iturbide. And there was no contact with the control tower before the plane suddenly disappeared from radar screens ten minutes after takeoff. Those are the only things we know for certain. Everything else was and is pure speculation. There were seven families desperately seeking the truth, and each of them believed in what gave their hearts the greatest amount of peace.

"Stop torturing yourselves. Our Chay is resting in peace. Let's leave the truth in God's hands," Tío Pete begged us.

Wise words. Nothing was going to bring back the mother, the sister or the daughter we'd lost. Nothing was going to bring back our Jacob, our Arturo, our Mario nor either of the two pilots. Not even the truth would be enough to ease this pain.

Arturo, Gigi and my dear Jacob had been working for my mother for years. My mother's success was theirs, and they shared in her pain, her joy, her laughter, her battles, her jokes. They would even share a glass of water. They were on that plane because they were a part of Jenni Rivera. I know she loved them, that she was passionate about them. They made sure that Jenni's engine was up and running each and every night.

I also know that my mother could be a very demanding boss, but when it came to birthdays or Christmas, she wouldn't allow anyone to buy presents for her team. That job belonged to her, and she didn't spare any expense. Nothing was too good for her team.

I don't know. Maybe it was time for all of them to go, together, as part of God's great plan, which we can't even begin to understand.

Even so, I ask the other six families for forgiveness if you felt at any moment that my mother was the cause of your pain, or if you felt she was the only one for whom tears were shed. My mother was just one member of this group, and they all deserve to be mourned equally. I keep you all in my prayers. I know that my mom is up there in heaven, surrounded by her best teammates.

Leaving aside that mess of investigations and lawsuits that some of the families of the victims filed, in the brand-new year of 2013, I would have to face a great hell of my own: how to survive in a house where I felt like an intruder.

∞

Since that beautiful message of "Don't worry" and "Don't back down" that I heard on the stage at her Celestial Graduation and that dream before Christmas where she embraced me, I hadn't felt either her warmth or her presence. My siblings dreamed about her all the time, and constantly felt her touch. But not me.

But that first night when we left the couch in favor of our own bedrooms, I felt it again.

That night, I turned out the light, and—worn-out from so many emotions—I called out to her. "Momma, where are you? I can't do this anymore; I can't deal with so much pain, so much guilt, so many new challenges that I have to face." That time I didn't hear her voice, but I felt her lay her hands on my head. She caressed me so gently that I was able to fall asleep like a baby. It was her way of saying to me, "Welcome home, this is where you belong, so don't feel bad. You never should have had to go, my princess."

I woke up with peace in my heart, ready to fight for my kids and work on ways we could go back to being a united family again. I wasn't about to let wills, documents or lawyers tell me what I had to do. No way!

The next night I went back to my bed hoping to feel her presence again, but there was nothing. I fell asleep without having her near me. Not that night, nor any other. After that one tender night, it seemed as if I was being shunned yet again.

"Dayanna, my mother has taken me back. I know it sounds crazy, but I can feel her energy in that house. When I go in her bedroom, I know that she's there," I desperately confessed to my friend. "I know she's watching over me—over all of us—and opening up good opportunities and things for our future, wherever she may be. Just like she's always done. But she's not reaching out to me!"

"Hmmm, sister." Dayanna thought. "I also feel that she has made peace with you, and that she isn't holding any grudges, and that she wants you to be in that house. But sometimes I wonder, have you really forgiven her, Chiquis?"

"I love her! I love her! I love her! There's no doubt about that!" I shouted, somewhat upset.

"Loving and forgiving aren't the same thing, sister," she said. And with that answer, my faithful friend got me thinking:

Oh, shit! I still felt resentment toward my mother. I was hurt because she left me in the middle of the worst chapter of my life, when it was she who could have written a happier ending. I remembered all those nights when she turned down my offer of a kiss or a hug, and it made me angry. Two months after she left us, and I was still blaming her for my pain and my problems, and that wasn't fair.

I felt like I couldn't breathe and I started to cry.

"I hate you and I love you, Momma. Why did you have to go like that? Why did you leave me like this? Why did you do this to me? Why didn't you just let me talk with you, hug you and kiss you, explain everything to you? Why? Why!"

Dayanna didn't know whether to hug me or grab me by the shoulders and shake the oncoming panic attack out of me.

"Listen, Chiquis. You forgave your father, you forgave so many people, so don't tell me that now you can't go and forgive your mother as well."

"You're absolutely right. I was even able to forgive Elena's girlfriend for having gotten caught up in the rumor mill that started this whole nightmare. I swear I forgave her months ago. The poor thing was pissed that Elena paid so much attention to my mother and me, and just got eaten up with jealousy. I'm not holding any grudges. We're all guilty of the sin of jealously at one point or another in this life, sister. But with my momma it's different . . . It's a thousand times stronger, and to top it all off, she's not here. How are we gonna fix this?" I answered, supremely frustrated.

"Look for her, sister. Look for the way. It's not impossible."

"Okay." I promised Dayanna that I would try, and I dried my tears with the sleeve of my pajamas. "Her pajamas!" I shouted.

"What are you talking about? Are you crazy?" Dayanna had really been spooked.

Suddenly I had remembered that that morning, Mercedes had come back to work with us at the house. Melele, as we affectionately call her, had been our loyal employee for many years. She cooked, cleaned, ironed, gave us the occasional scolding and told us stories about when she was young and used to fight with her sisters-in-law. And Melele loved to do the laundry!

I ran down to the kitchen and there was our Melele, with a mop and chlorine in hand.

"Melele, don't touch my momma's bedroom!" I said desperately.

"But, *mija*, the dust is up to here!"

"No. Leave the sheets and covers exactly the way they are. And don't wash her clothes."

The two of us went upstairs, and as soon as we entered her room, Melele tried to negotiate with me.

"Okay, Chiquis, I won't touch the bed or the clothes. But you have to let me dust."

"Fine, but just a little bit," I agreed. "But don't touch those pajamas there at the foot of the bed."

Melele gave me a hug, and that's when I saw the tears welling up in her eyes.

"Oh, Melele, how are we ever gonna get through this?" I said as we held each other in our arms.

But I already knew the answer. The only way was through forgiveness.

23.

THE DAMN VIDEO

"Cuz, it's time to see it."

I went in my mother's office and stared at the enormous desk there in the middle of the room. The seat was empty. Nobody felt strong enough to fill that position quite yet.

"See what, Chiquis?" my mother's cousin Tere asked while she was organizing some papers off in a corner.

During those last few months of my mother's life, Tere had been acting as her secretary. We needed her help to finish up some things that had been left half done. And I, more than anyone, needed to close up what had been left open for me.

"The video, *prima*. The video."

"But why, Chiquis? Don't do this to yourself. It's over now. Everyone's forgotten all about it."

"That's a lie. The public hasn't forgotten about it. I'm still getting insulted on Twitter. And every time I see my aunts and uncles, I still don't think they're convinced of my innocence. They say they believe me, but I still have my doubts and that's no way to live!"

"Okay, then, here it is. Now you'll know . . ." With hesitation, she opened a desk drawer and took out a tiny black USB drive and handed it to me.

My hand was shaking when I took it. Finally, here it was: the damn video that had caused me so much pain. Only my mother, her stylist and friend Vanessa and Tere had seen it. Not even Tía Rosie had had the opportunity. Every time Rosie asked my mother to watch it, my mother came up with some excuse.

I went straight to the computer and opened the file. It took me four hours to review each and every second of footage taken by three separate cameras on that fateful night: one from my mother's closet, one from the hallway that leads to my mother's bedroom, and one from the main entrance to the house. Nothing. Nobody. Empty hallways, empty spaces. I saw the top of my head while I was sitting on the stairs talking on the phone to my tío Juan and my boyfriend. I saw myself going in her room to say good night to Esteban, and I saw myself leaving, completely normally, just five minutes later. I saw myself walking out through the front door, and two minutes later, Esteban came down to turn out the lights before returning to his bedroom.

Half an hour after I left—on the camera my mother installed in her closet to keep watch over her safe—you can just barely make out Esteban heading in the direction of the bathroom. A little while later, he walks back, this time wrapped up in towels. For obvious reasons, there were no cameras in the actual bedroom itself. And the view inside the closet was cloaked in darkness. The light from the nearby bathroom was all that illuminated it.

After Esteban got out of the shower, there were hours and hours of absolutely nothing.

"Prima, I'm in shock. Where did she come up with this story based on this video? There is nothing here, just as I have told everybody all along," I said to Tere.

"I know, but I don't want you obsessing over this video the way your mother did. She spent hours going over it. And she told me, 'You see? You see that shadow? That's Chiquis; she came back to the house and snuck back into the bedroom.' But I swear to you, I didn't see anything like that."

"Why didn't you say anything?" I demanded angrily.

"Chiquis, I'm sorry. I tried to, but she got so mad at me that I was afraid she'd fire me."

My family stayed silent, and the bullies and haters continued to tear me apart on social media. There were even some journalists who must have been hallucinating because they spoke as if they had seen the damn video with their own eyes: "Here you can see Chiquis buttoning her blouse as she leaves, and Esteban pulling up his pants, his dark-colored jeans," I heard one report say. Another one seemed to know all the details, because it reported that, "What you see here is a threesome with her mom's friend Elena." Not even out of respect for the memory of my mother—may she rest in peace—would they refrain from talking all this bullshit.

That same day, I called my grandma and said, "*Abuelita*, this Sunday, I want everyone here at the house. Help me get everyone together. It's about time they gave me the opportunity to speak. I've been denied that chance for a whole year now."

My grandma Rosa agreed to convince everyone to attend. This just couldn't go on any longer. I needed to tell them my version of the events, and explain how my mother had made a tragic and terrible mistake.

That afternoon, the entire family was together for the first time since the day of the funeral. And they sat down to watch that infamous video. Nobody could make it to the end of the recording. They'd lose interest, they'd get up to use the bathroom, or they'd just talk amongst themselves. Part of me thought that they didn't want to watch it, because then they would feel guilty for how horribly they'd treated me during those days. Obviously, nobody saw anything that was cause for alarm, and no one could understand where such rumors could have come from.

I also took the opportunity to show them the evidence I had gathered for my mother. I first showed them my phone bill statements, so they could see for themselves who I was talking with on the stairs, what time I left the house, what time I got to my apartment and what time I called my boyfriend before going to sleep. How I wish I could have shown those cell phone records to my mother. Ever since the scandal broke, the only thing I wanted was for her to just listen to me. My mother was never able to do that, but at least the rest of my family could, even if it was too late.

"Chiquis," my tío Pete said, his voice filled with love and tenderness, "we don't care about that video. Forgive us if we ever doubted you. It's clear you could never do such a thing. We love you, Chiquis."

Everything was all hugs and kisses, and I appreciated it. For the first time in quite a while, I felt supported, respected and loved. But even so, I still wasn't quite satisfied. Nobody doubted me, but nor was anyone willing to step up and defend my reputation publicly.

"Okay, Chiquis, it's true. There's no physical evidence, despite what your mother swore," Tía Rosie explained to me. "But how does that matter anymore? She's no longer with us. Why keep pushing?"

I couldn't believe it. They were still afraid of her, even after she was gone! They'd rather leave me swimming with the sharks than contradict my deceased mother. Incredible!

Maybe, if I were able to piece together all the bits of rumor, I'd be able to remove the proverbial scarlet "A" from my chest, the

215

mark that was suffocating me and keeping me from moving forward with my life. If I could complete the puzzle, I thought, I could earn the forgiveness of the fans, and—more importantly—I might even be able to forgive my mother. That was something I really needed to feel. She was watching over me and guiding me, but from a distance. A very long distance. And every time a cousin or sibling said they dreamed about her or felt her presence in a certain song, I would be dying of envy. I had to forgive her, and in order to do that, I had to understand.

∞

"Vanessa, how are you?" When she heard my voice, it took her a couple of seconds to answer.

"Good, good, Chiquis. What a surprise. And you?"

Vanessa—my mother's stylist and closest friend during the last few months of her life, the one who almost choked me with a look back during Jenicka's *quinceañera*—was the only one who could help me complete my double mission: get that scarlet letter off my chest, and get me to feel my mother's presence again, even if it was only in my dreams.

"I need to see you," I said. "Please, you're the only one who can help get me out of this."

Vanessa had greeted me at my mother's graduation ceremony, and given me a reconciling hug, but we both knew that there was a conversation we still needed to have.

"Of course, Chiquis. I was thinking it was time for us to talk as well. Come over to my house. I'll cook up something delicious."

That's just how we Mexicans are. No open, heart-to-heart conversations without some food on the table. A good beef or chicken stew can fix everything. Even the strongest enemies of the past will crumble like *queso fresco*.

"First, Chiquis, I want to apologize. I also watched that video your mother had, and I didn't see anything suspicious. Forgive me, but I just didn't know how to convince her," she told me, her voice choked up with tears as soon as I got to her house. I squeezed her hand tightly from across the table so she could feel my love. I wasn't there to pass judgment or interrogate her. All I wanted to do was relive my mother's last few days through her eyes and her memories.

Vanessa was the last person my mother spoke with before heading off for Monterrey. If anyone could help me solve this mystery, it was her.

"Your mom insisted that after Esteban got in the shower, you snuck back into the house without turning on any of the lights and hid in the closet, waiting for him to come out of the bathroom. And that's how it happened. There was no debating it; she was very adamant about it," Vanessa said, detailing each and every one of my mother's words and reactions. "And I told her, 'Jen, if they knew there was a camera right there in that corner of the closet, why would they pick that place to do it? They're not idiots. They could have done it in the bedroom, where there aren't any cameras at all. Of all the places in your home, the closet is under the most surveillance.' And you can just imagine how your mother reacted to that. She was on a rampage! I didn't want to fight her on it."

"But did you at least try to talk some sense into her?" I asked.

"Yes, twice, and on both occasions she flew into a rage. One night, on our way back home from the airport after missing a flight, she cried and cried behind the wheel, saying, 'I can't believe it, my own daughter . . .' So I asked her again: 'Are you sure, Jen? Because I just don't see it . . .' Your mother started pounding her fists on the steering wheel; she was furious, and she shouted at me, 'If you don't believe me, then fuck you and fuck them . . . You're just like all the rest, all those sons of bitches . . . If you don't believe me, then why are you trying to be my friend?'"

Vanessa paused and started to cry again. Those memories hurt her as much as they hurt me. Then she continued:

"So after that, I said, *Fuck it! If my friend wants to be wrong, then fine, but I'm not going to lose her, I'm not going to leave her on her own. Better just to keep my mouth shut.* But then, everyone started pouring more and more fuel on the fire, and I swear I even started to believe it myself. Then all the suck-ups started saying, 'Oh yeah, I always thought something was going on, I saw them talking in secret . . . I saw them getting out of a car . . . I saw them doing this, I saw them doing that.' Those asslickers, as you call them, turned suspicion into reality. What started in your mother's mind ended up on everybody's lips."

"But why, Vanessa? Why would family and friends want to cause so much harm?" It was hard for me to understand how the evil in some people could spread so far.

"Nothing, Chiquis, other than to gain favor with your mother. And I suppose there are one or two who were happy to see you separated and estranged. When you were at the house, everything was all, Chiquis Chiquis Chiquis, and your mother consulted with you on everything. But after the split, they were happy you weren't influencing things, and that she was leaning more on them."

"That's awful, Vanessa. I swear, all this fame has come at a heavy price. But didn't my momma realize what was going on?"

"No, Chiquis. At the time, your mother wasn't the same, she wasn't her usual self. She was lonely, so lonely; she was in an emotional place where nobody could reach her. I think Jenni was going through a stage where she just felt exhausted and thought that the whole world had failed her, or robbed her, or betrayed her. I think stress hit her really hard. The stress of working fifteen years without a break, fifteen years of planes, hotels, shows, concerts, perfume, tequila, television shows and a thousand different business endeavors. And to top it all off, your mother was on a very strict diet, she wasn't sleeping much, and when you walk around hungry and tired it's easy to get all pissed off and blow up at the smallest thing. She was irritable, and snapped at every little thing. My poor Jen, she just couldn't handle it anymore, and as usual, there was the family, bitching and moaning with their arguments, and her brothers were always causing her problems."

"Yes, I remember back then she wasn't speaking with my tío Lupe," I interrupted.

"That's just it, Chiquis. She told me she was tired of being the police officer, keeping everyone from fighting and not getting anyone angry because she gave more to one of them than the others. And you all at the house, you had her on her last nerves. Johnny with his antics, Jacqie with her pregnancy, Mikey and the fallout with that underage girl, and you, Chiquis, you were the one she suffered the most with."

"But how? If I was the one who helped out the most and worked the hardest?"

"Because of your boyfriend, Chiquis. Jenni and your boyfriend were on an equal playing field when it came to competing for your attention. She felt that he wasn't the right man for you, and jealousy was eating her up inside because he was going to take you away from her. This guy wasn't like your other boyfriends, who would obey her every word."

"I know she was on hormone therapy for a year," I mentioned. "Who knows, maybe that affected her too."

"I think it was mostly stress. My poor friend and those ghosts from the past that always seem to creep back into her life. Your mother never forgot how much the men in her life had made her suffer, along with what happened with you and Rosie. It's all tied together. And with Esteban, she felt defeated. She didn't love him and didn't want to admit to the world that yet another marriage was going to hell. Just one more failure! Yes, the great Diva was a huge success onstage, but when it came to her personal life, she felt as if everything was going down the drain. She isolated herself so much emotionally that not even her best friends were able to get inside her heart. It was solitude: that's what was eating away at her, Chiquis."

"I understand her suffering, but I still don't see why she took it all out on me."

"Me either. It was too much. Even after filing for divorce, she still spoke with Esteban. He even came to the house to collect a few things and she was sweet to him. I kept asking myself, why doesn't her own daughter get that same opportunity to speak, even over the phone?"

Suddenly it hit me, and a huge smile lit up my face, much to Vanessa's surprise.

"Chiquis, that should really bother you, that he was on speaking terms with her and you weren't."

"No, no, you don't understand, Vanessa. You just confirmed the one thing that mattered most to me: that my mother never really believed that I slept with Esteban."

"Huh? I don't understand."

"She might have somewhat believed it in her head, but not in her heart. I know her. You know her too. If she really believed it, she never would have let Esteban come pick up his things. She would have burned them all out in the yard like she did with Juan. She never would have let him near that house. You know my momma!"

"Wow, you're right!" Vanessa said, suddenly seeing it too. "She would have fucked him up and she would have kicked your ass. I'm sorry, but your mother never would have let you out of her life without giving you a couple good slaps to the face."

"Exactly! So my mother didn't leave this world thinking I'm a whore. That's enough for me."

"And there's more, Chiquis," Vanessa said, her eyes filling up with tears once again. "Your mother was at my house on Thanksgiving when Rosie forwarded her your e-mail. She read it in front of me, on her BlackBerry. And while she was reading it, she couldn't stop crying. I said, 'Listen, Esteban is just one more man, but your daughter is your daughter. I want you to answer this question, and be completely honest with me: If your daughter did sleep with Esteban, would you forgive her?' Your mother bowed her head and said, very softly, 'Yes.' And if she never slept with Esteban, would you ask her to forgive you for what you've done? And without lifting her head, she answered again, 'Yes, but I need just a little more time. Give me some time.'"

"Damn time. Fucking time. We never had enough!" I felt rage coursing through my veins. Rage against life itself, which took her away from me before her time. That was all my mother had asked for: time. And that was the one thing she was never granted.

"Don't be angry, Chiquis. That was what God wanted. It was His will," Vanessa replied, interjecting some calmness.

"I know, I know, but it still hurts. It's hard for me to accept that. She was trying to teach me a lesson, in a very strange way. And now I understand, Vanessa. She was losing me and couldn't bear it. I know she was going to let me back into her life and that she just wanted to teach me a lesson, just like the first time she stopped talking to me for two months when I was fourteen. It was a lesson from a mother to her daughter, to let me know how much it would hurt to lose her. That was it, Vanessa. I can see it all so clearly now. I wasn't the best daughter, and I didn't make it easy for her, I admit."

"I know," Vanessa said. "I could see for myself how much you loved each other and how much you hated one another at the same time. Jenni was jealous, I won't deny that, but you were too. And with the two of you being so close in age, it couldn't have been easy living under the same roof with another woman and not compete over the silliest things: jeans, girlfriends, jokes. You were both really bitchy toward each other—I heard how each of you spoke—but you couldn't live without each other."

"Yes, that's true, everyone in this family can get jealous. Seriously jealous! We're just like any other family: the little one is jealous of the bigger one, and the bigger one is jealous of the little one. But I swear, we all love each other so much!"

"But this time the jealousy had been building up, and there was a man in the middle of it. I noticed it when you went out to eat with Esteban and the kids at Las Islitas. Your mother wasn't too happy about that. And she didn't like leaving Esteban alone with her assistant Julie. I don't know. Life had left her jealous when it came to men. It wasn't her fault. They've betrayed her time and time again, and they've done much worse."

Three bowls of soup and three hours later, we finally got to the heart of the issue:

"There's no doubt about it," Vanessa insisted. "It was exhaustion, it was jealousy, it was stress and it was those damn rumors. All just stewing in that pressure cooker of hers. But I swear, she cried over you, and never stopped loving you. Not even for a second."

"Thanks, Vanessa. I can't thank you enough for everything you've said to me. Now, if you would just tell me this: that final night with her, I want to know what she did, what she said, what she ate. Everything!"

"It was the Thursday before the accident. She came by the salon to surprise me; she was wearing all black with a lovely hat and a great pair of boots, and she asked me to go to the mall with her. We went to Topanga; we laughed, we talked and we went through all the stores. I never saw her spend so much money. She bought Christmas presents for all her employees in Mexico and for your cousins. Twenty-five thousand dollars in a couple of hours. Then we went back to her house; she fixed me some *huevos rancheros,* and then we went up to her room so I could help her pack. She had to be at the airport in just a couple of hours and be on the way to her last two concerts. 'I think I'll take all my most expensive jewelry,' she said. 'Why?' I asked. 'Because they're mine, hahaha!' she replied, and looked at me as if to say, 'Fuck it!'

"After we were done picking out the dresses and shoes for her to wear for the two shows, we stood there looking at the two massive pieces of luggage. Your mother was exhausted. She propped her foot up against the wall, shrugged her shoulders and after a deep sigh she told me, 'After this trip, it's over, girlfriend. I'm tired of this shit. Why don't you sleep here tonight.' I said that I couldn't because I had to work early the next morning. And with that, she lay down on the bed and curled up like a little ball under the covers. It broke my heart to see her like that."

Vanessa was a little choked up, remembering her friend curled up on that enormous bed, remembering all that grief, and she had to take a deep breath before being able to continue:

"I stroked her hair and said, 'Don't worry, everything is going to be alright. You come back on Tuesday, right?' Your mother responded without words, with her eyes closed and barely nodded yes. That kinda freaked me out. I gave her a kiss on the forehead and said, 'Okay, I love you, bye,' as I turned out the lights. As I was leaving her room, I heard her say, 'I love you too,' in the softest voice. I felt that I was leaving her very much alone. In that house filled with people who loved her, at the height of her fame, with thousands of adoring fans . . . and yet alone. I stood outside of her door for a few minutes and something just didn't feel right. It felt like that was the last time I was going to see her. I should have just stayed with her."

"Don't blame yourself, Vanessa. You did what you could. I'll always be grateful to you for being there for her, through the good times and the bad. Thank you."

It was time to get up from the table and say good night. The memories and the confessions had left us both completely exhausted, but with much peace in our hearts.

"Forgive me, Chiquis. Again, I'm so sorry that I judged you instead of defending you," she repeated, giving me one last hug. "I wish we had spoken sooner. I would have found a way to fix all this. The lesson I learned is that from now on, I should always follow my instincts and not stay quiet, because who knows if we'll be here tomorrow to share that one last *I love you*. I love you, Chiquis."

"I love you too, Vanessa."

I jumped in my car. It was already dark, and the cold February air was still hanging on to that part of the San Fernando Valley. And I thought, as I was driving back to Encino, that in the aftermath of that colossal nonsense, things were finally all starting to make sense.

24.

HAPPY BIRTHDAY, MOM

I'm not asking for jewels
Or furs or palaces . . .

Sitting there, during the flight from New York to Los Angeles,
I couldn't get that song by my mother out of my head. Six months
after she left us, it was the only one I could listen to without bursting into tears. And I still couldn't watch any of her videos.

I hope you understood
That I am desperate . . .

Every verse spoke to me, every chorus was dedicated to me,
the pariah, the poor little princess, unwelcome in her mother's
castle, and still, it never kept me up at night. My desperation came
from somewhere else.

I had just cohosted *The View*, alongside some of the great leg-
ends of journalism and entertainment like Barbara Walters and
Whoopi Goldberg. And, of course, Barbara was not cruel in the

225

least. She handled the issues of family abuse and the loss of my mother with such delicacy and elegance that any nervousness I felt simply vanished as soon as I looked into her eyes.

That same week, I had been offered two other very tempting television projects. It was clear that my mother was watching over me and opening doors for me. I wasn't completely alone, but there was still that chilly sense of distance between the two of us.

Her birthday was coming up, along with my own and that of my tía Rosie. The first time I would spend them without her. So I just dreamed about her. I dreamed about her during those days in New York. And in those dreams, she neither kissed me nor hugged me. She seemed very tired, looked ragged and unkempt, was very thin and she told me that she wasn't dead, she'd been kidnapped. I can't quite explain it, but she seemed somehow lovely in the midst of all that pain. In one dream she said, "Don't sell the house. I know you're under pressure, I know the house scares you and that it's worth a lot of money, but don't sell it, Chiquis. I'm with you there. You're going to be fine." I tried to move toward her, but no matter what I did, she always seemed to remain at the same distance. Such a weird dream! But like in the previous instances, she seemed calm, at peace, with an immense love for me, while still just out of reach.

It was just a short dream, but it confirmed for me that she was still showing me the way. *Maybe our plan of having you manage my career is being fulfilled in this strange way, Momma,* I thought to myself as I leaned back in my seat on the flight home. As soon as we landed, there was another difficult task awaiting me: our attorneys had informed us that Trino, my father, had filed an appeal to his sentence. He'd be appearing before a judge, and I would have to be present there as well, whether I liked it or not.

In one of life's great ironies, the date of the appearance was set for June 26: my birthday. *Does he remember?* I wondered as I sat down on those cold, wooden benches.

A few minutes later, he entered the courtroom through one of the side doors. He was handcuffed and wearing his orange jumpsuit, and accompanied by two court officers. He looked old, worn-out, with a lot of gray hair and a huge belly. Clearly his days as a dashing young man were behind him. His attitude, however, had not changed: he never turned to look at me, and his body language was arrogant. Suddenly I realized that my feelings about him had, in fact, changed: I still didn't hate him, and my forgiveness was constant, but I no longer felt sorry for him. And I didn't feel a need for him to accept me, speak to me or even look at me.

There were so many times when I tried to get in touch with both him and his family, and yet every time I was denied. On the other hand, since my mother's passing, his family had started inviting Jacqie to Marín family gatherings, and she even became friends with our stepbrother, Dora's son. Meanwhile, I was still being ignored and it hurt. Still, though, I learned that my grandpa Trinidad was very ill, and that he was nearing the end. I didn't care how anyone looked at it: I went straight to the home of one of my aunts and gave him a kiss. My grandpa had always been good to me, and nobody could deny me the right to say good-bye to him.

That day, much to my surprise, everyone smiled and visited with me, and one of my aunts even whispered in my ear: "Chiquis, get ready, because soon your father is going to want to see you. Very soon, in fact." Suddenly I saw it for what it was: a layer of sweet words with an ulterior motive underneath. A lot of sweet words, in fact, but nobody had the decency to ask about my mother. Four weeks after the accident, and still nobody had the guts to even ask me, "How are you feeling, Chiquis? We're so sorry about what happened." It made my stomach turn, and I got out of that house before all that artificial sugar made me sick.

And there, sitting in that same Long Beach courthouse where, five years earlier, we had waged the great battle of our lives, I understood why my aunts were trying to sweeten me up and why my father was so arrogantly asking the judge to reduce the twenty-six years of his sentence that were still ahead of him: because his number one enemy—the one he feared the most—was no longer there to oppose him! Good God! Dolores Janney Rivera, his archenemy, was gone, and that emboldened them all.

But that morning, with or without my mother's presence here in this world, the judge denied his appeal. Simple and quick. No.

She might not be here to testify before this judge, but she's sitting there, in a much higher court, next to a much more powerful judge, I said to myself when the gavel came crashing down.

As the guards were escorting him back to his cell, I thought, *May God watch over you, Dad.*

That came straight from my heart. For what he did to me as a little girl, I forgave him a thousand times. But it would be a betrayal of my mother if I sought out the friendship of a man who never even sent me a message of condolence, who in fact seemed to revel in our misery.

A week later, we celebrated my mom's birthday. And with that day came a gift for everyone: her autobiography, *Unbreakable*, was released, and it quickly became a huge bestseller. I have to admit, though, that to this day I have only read a few pages. I just can't. The sadness clouds my eyes every time I try to read more.

For that first birthday without her, we decided to get the whole Rivera family together in the backyard for a simple little family ceremony. Melele insisted of me:

"Chiquis, why don't you wear your mother's printed dress. Don't be a party pooper. It's there in the closet. Just put it on."

To make her happy, I went up and changed into that long, cheerful and very comfortable dress that my momma loved to wear for family festivities, and I went back down to rejoin my siblings. They all smiled when they saw me. And though the memories were eating us alive, no tears were shed. Between the laughter and jokes, and after a lovely prayer, we released some white balloons into the sky that contained messages and hopes. Mine read, *Please, Momma, guide me so that I can raise our babies how you would want me to. And please help me to forgive you.*

That balloon floated higher . . . and higher . . . until it became a tiny white dot over the Encino hills. Then it was lost in the immense blue sky over the valley. As I looked to the heavens I thought:

If I could forgive my father, after all the harm he caused; if I could forgive that other woman; if I could forgive my mother's fans, who hurt me so deeply; if I could forgive Esteban for not being man enough to clear everything up; if I could forgive my family for doubting me and not defending me . . . why can't I forgive you, Momma? With all the love I have for you, why can't I do it? Why does it hurt so much that you left without giving me a hug, without retracting the accusations, without giving me a kiss? My heart is still broken.

Then, searching the clouds for that tiny white dot in hopes of seeing it one more time, I was reminded of the expression, "There's a thin line between love and hate." Two emotions so near and yet so far apart. Like the yin and the yang. And in between, my mother and me, and that damn forgiveness that continued to elude me.

25.

"WHITE DOVE"

The months and years on the calendar raced by, and we found ourselves in January of 2014. How time flies. It was Friday, a cold Friday, sometime after eight in the evening, and I got in the truck, alone. I didn't want anyone coming with me. All I had was a bottle of La Gran Señora tequila. I was wearing sweatpants and a pair of Uggs. And I drove off in the direction of my new life: recording my first song.

I'd made the decision months before: restart the plans to get into singing as soon as the first anniversary of the accident was behind us.

We celebrated that anniversary at the very same arena in Monterrey where my mother gave her final performance before boarding that damn plane. It was really hard to see, for the first time, the airport where she took off early that Sunday morning. It was hard driving down that same road to her hotel. But all the Riveras were there, surrounded by the insurmountable affection of her fans. Thousands of voices shouting, "Jenni *vive!*" I introduced a couple of the artists during that tribute, and a couple of my uncles and siblings were moved to sing. Even my tío Lupe, who'd said he wasn't going to come, showed up at the last minute, putting aside the conflicts he was having with his brothers.

But what I remember most is the intense feeling of love that my mother was sending us through her fans. When the crowd was chanting, "Chiquis!" or "Rosie!" or "Jacqie!" it was as if my mother was telling us, "I'm here, and I love you." She was present, yes, but just a couple of little steps behind me. My mother still wasn't quite standing beside me.

When the event was over, I stood there staring out at the half-empty stadium, watching the people leaving, and I closed my eyes and prayed: "I miss you Momma, I know you were here, and that you're listening. Now I'm the one who is asking you for time. Give me time to fix everything in my heart."

A month later, here I was, on my way to the studio with the lyrics to "Paloma Blanca" in hand, thinking that this would be the night and this would be the song. I wrote these verses to put an end to my anger and my pain. My mother liked to put an end to our fights by dedicating songs, and so I would do the same.

Fausto Juarez, the producer and engineer, was waiting for me there at the studio. I had given explicit orders that no one else could be present. I asked him to lower the lights, I took two shots of my mother's tequila and I cried. I cried a lot.

Fly high, fly free
Fly, my white dove
And though you are not here with me
I will live beneath your wings . . .

And I sang . . . I sang a lot there in that isolated and almost dark recording booth.

231

I had so much to tell you
But you wouldn't let me
I'm going to tear out the pain with the love that you left me . . .

I sang it three times in a row, start to finish, stopping only to wipe away my tears.

I may have been wrong
But it never was about all of that
It's not a part of this world
To betray the one I love most . . .

And I thought, after that last shot, that the forgiveness I so coveted would surround me. I thought that was the time when God would allow my wound to finally heal.

I'm going to pray in your name
I'm going to ask that you rest
I feel that your soul can hear me
So let us finally make peace . . .

But no. Nothing. I left the record with Fausto and left the studio disheartened. My emotions were running around like crazy.

Sitting in my truck, watching the headlights of the cars coming down Ventura Boulevard, I shouted, "God, I'm begging you! I have to shake off this pain before it breaks me down. If time cures everything, then what is happening to me?"

While I was still trying to find peace, there were others who were starting to feel the effects of time.

"Chiquis, your tío Juan and I think it's time we repaid our debt to you," Tía Rosie said, standing in my bedroom door. Right away,

I knew this was something important. She, her husband and her two daughters lived on the first floor of the house, and rarely went up to the second floor, where Mikey, Johnny, Jenicka and I had our bedrooms. Without ever actually saying so, each family had settled into its own little corner of that enormous home. Together, yet still separate.

"Juan and I decided that we would give an interview this weekend to clear your name and to explain to the world that you never had anything to do with Esteban," my aunt said in a serious voice. The decision had been made.

"Okay . . ." I replied, a bit suspicious. "If that's what you want, then go right ahead. Right now I have bigger problems to deal with, and the truth and public opinion are old news. It's been two years since the scandal broke, tía. But if that's what you feel you need to do, then more power to you. Just one question: Why now?"

"Chiquis, because now I know how you felt all along. I don't know how you were able to go on living in the midst of all that public humiliation and bullying," she said.

I could see that Rosie was on the verge of tears, and suddenly I understood: ever since she took over Jenni Rivera Enterprises as executor, people had done nothing but tear her down. "She's skimming money off the top, she's a selfish old witch, she charges interview fees, she lives for free in her dead sister's house but charges Chiquis rent." Now she knew firsthand what it was like to be the name on the tip of everybody's tongue, to be the center of envy and rumors, and she didn't like it. She looked exhausted, and I couldn't blame her. Taking over everything my mother left behind is a hell of a task. Only Jenni knew how to deal with so many responsibilities, criticisms and obstacles at once. And even Super Jenni, the strongest of us all, got worn-out and fell from the sky.

"I'm sorry, Chiquis, for not standing up and defending you. My love for my sister stopped me. Defending you would be to publically admit that my sister was wrong, and I didn't feel like I had the strength to tarnish her memory. I just couldn't do it, after losing her in such a tragic way. But now it's time."

Said and done. They had already planned how they would be doing it. Rosie and Juan would be sitting down with Myrka Dellanos, and would give their exclusive. *Oh well,* I thought. *At least it will be with a woman like Myrka, who will know how to treat the issue with dignity.*

"Thank you, tía. I'm grateful. Better late than never. But I'm not expecting much to come from this. It'll be whatever God wants it to be," I replied, and gave her a hug.

Our relationship during that year hadn't been an easy one. We had our little issues, which was to be expected, after all the emotional and legal pressure we'd had to bear. She had the title, but I was doing the work as mother and housewife. My younger siblings and I had our way of doing things, and she and her family had theirs. But I know we were both trying to do the right thing each and every day, just as my mother would have wanted us to do.

So that's how it was. My tío Juan and my tía Rosie gave their interview, and somehow—after seeing them and listening to their words—I was able to forgive them for delaying it for so long. Although, as I'd thought, their statements had little effect on the public, and little effect on my heart, which for all intents and purposes was still at war.

The peace I was searching for came to me shortly after that, though via a different path. It came through a major screwup on my part. I had to do something pretty damn bad before I hit rock bottom and was able to find my mother once again.

Finally, "Paloma Blanca" was released on just about every radio station in the country. I swear, I never even heard the final master cut that was ultimately released and sent out. And immediately my Twitter feed caught fire with the most horrendous comments:

You fucking hack, you can't sing. This song sucks. You're just riding your mother's fame. You wanna be like Jenni but you never will.

Oh no! More harassment! I was crushed. I broke down. But I have to admit that the insults—after being called a bitch so many times in the past—didn't hurt as much. This time, what hurt was having screwed up with the very song that was supposed to have been a form of medicine between mother and daughter.

In my defense, I will say that it's a difficult song, with a lot of fluctuation between the bass and the treble, and we didn't do a bad job as a team. But the cut that was released on the radio was not the one that should have been published. It was a strategic mistake. I never had the chance to correctly master the song.

"We'll rerelease it," was the producer's immediate response.

"No. If we screwed it up, then that's it. Please, don't even mess with it," I asked in a fit of honesty. One thing we all learned from my mother is to face up to your mistakes, not to run away from them.

I went home and spent the next few days reading all the highly opinionated messages. Some of them were true: as a singer, I had a long way to go. But internally I tried to find encouragement: when my mother first started singing, she was only so-so, but she ended up learning how to develop her voice and her style. I know that one day I'll get there too.

And when I started getting those tweets, like "You're just riding your mother's fame, you're just trying to be like her," it made me want to yell to the world: "Of course I want to be like her! I'm her daughter! Didn't you grow up emulating your parents? Didn't you want to walk like them and talk like them? Who the hell do you want me to be like instead, Celine Dion?"

And when it comes to riding my mother's fame, that has never been my intention. However, in a weird way, it was her wish and she repeated it a thousand times over: "I'm building a name, a brand you can benefit from, that you can carry forward," she would say. I'm tired of explaining and justifying the reasons why I started singing. It was something I'd been talking about and planning with my mother for years. And this was the time to make it a reality. Period.

Music runs through the Rivera family veins. We were born and raised around instruments and microphones. It's what my grandpa taught all of us. I don't understand why the whole world seems surprised that now I want to start singing as well. It would be stranger if I wanted to be a scuba diver or a nurse, wouldn't it? Music was always there in my heart, but the moment wasn't always right. But now is the time.

∞

I grabbed my phone, sent out a giant *"WHATEVER"* dedicated to all the haters comparing me to my mother and went to bed. I spent three sleepless nights in a row, but on the third—between the frustration and the exhaustion—it happened.

It was three in the morning. I'm a bit obsessed about that time of day, I admit. It's when her plane took off. I got up to get a glass of water, and suddenly I felt an overwhelming need to pray. I got down on my knees and spoke first with God. Then, I turned to my mother, and from my mouth came these words:

"Momma, I'm sorry, I'm so sorry if I ever made you feel like you weren't a good mother, like you weren't good enough for me. Please forgive me, as I forgive you. I forgive you for having left me with this pain, I forgive you, Momma, I forgive you."

I couldn't believe it myself, but it was coming from my heart.

"I forgive you for everything you did that made me cry, and for doubting me. I forgive you for denying me a good-bye hug and kiss."

At this point, the tears took over, and I gave in. But it wasn't a painful cry, it was a healing one.

"I know that you did everything to make me into a stronger person. And I am. I swear to you, I am. I learned the lesson. Now I want to be happy, and carry you with me in my heart. I want you to guide me with the kids, and with my career. You knew how to fall, how to get back up and how to get better each and every day. I need you to help me get out of this, so that I can continue to sing to you, and to sing in your honor. Only your love will carry me forward. I love you, Momma, and I miss you."

No sooner had I spoken those words than my tears stopped, and I felt the strange sensation that my mother had accepted my prayers and my forgiveness. I didn't hear her voice, but I did feel her warmth on my face and in my heart. And a silence filled with peace and happiness surrounded both me and the entire rest of the house.

I went back to bed and slept like a baby. It was the kind of sleep I hadn't had in years. It was peaceful and silent. I didn't dream about her, or anyone, or anything. My soul was exhausted, but blessed.

The next morning, when I opened my eyes, I felt her there. My mother was next to me, very close, and she stayed beside me with every step I took. I went downstairs, entered the kitchen, went out into the yard. There she was, right there with me. She wasn't shutting me out any longer. And all I could do was smile.

"I did it, sister," I told Dayanna on the phone a few days later.

"You got custody?" she replied, on the other end of the line. She knew that sooner or later I was going to file for legal custody of Johnny and Jenicka.

"No, sister. I forgave her. I forgave my mother, and I feel like the happiest woman on earth. I swear, I forgave her a hundred and ten percent."

I just couldn't contain my joy, and I knew that Dayanna was one of the few people who would understand.

"Oh my God! Finally! You had me worried. I could see you suffering, sister. I could see it in your eyes."

"Yeah, the whole 'Paloma Blanca' mess really touched my soul. I think I felt the way my mother must have felt back in the beginning, when nobody believed in her and everyone just laughed at her. How ironic! Only when I put myself in her shoes was I able to forgive her. That's the best way to say it."

"Chiquis, she never left your shoes. It was you who kept her at a distance. But that's over now. I'm so happy. Now go put on those stilettos and walk strong!"

"I promise I will, sister. I'm gonna keep on singing, and fuck what they think about me. And yes, I'm gonna fight for custody too. Now I feel strong enough."

"Yes, well, for that you're gonna need more than just a prayer, sister," Dayanna said, laughing. "May God and a couple of good lawyers give you their blessings!"

Blessings! If that's what it's all about, the first blessing I would need would be from Rosie. I didn't want to get into a legal battle with my own family.

"Why, Chiquis?" she asked me when I brought up my intentions. "Do you think I'm not doing a good enough job?"

"No, tía, that's not it. It's just that the kids and I talked. They agree. Johnny wants to know why I'm not fighting for them."

"Okay, it's just a piece of paper, Chiquis. I never wanted to take your place, but if that would make them happy, then I won't oppose it. I'll never fight for something that belongs to you. And the kids have always been yours."

That was the green light and the blessing I needed.

A few days after our conversation, I met up with Rosie again, this time at the office where she was waiting with her attorneys and the documents, which had already been signed. As I walked into the room, I overheard what they were saying:

"Don't worry, as executor, you will still control the money."

"No, it's fine, I'm not worried about that," I interjected, completely at peace. "All I want is what's mine: the children."

I don't think that people understood that I was happy being disinherited. In fact, I feel that my mother did me a great favor. If she had left me with millions in the bank, I think I would have lain down in bed and cried, and I would have sunk deeper into depression. Not having life all planned out left me with no other choice but to go out and fight each and every morning to earn my bread. I make every dollar I have. I'm a hardworking woman, just like my mother was her entire life. And thanks to that, I can honestly say that I wake up every morning feeling proud of exactly who I am.

With nothing else to discuss, I signed the custody papers, and all that was left was to wait for the judge, who was running a few minutes late.

Meanwhile, with or without the legal status, I continued to play the mother role there in Encino. A mom who occasionally had to get tough. Raising two teenagers is no easy task. "Chiquis, don't get mad, but Esteban invited me to Universal Studios, and I want to go see him." Johnny was asking permission, hoping to see his best friend and sports hero. I knew he'd texted our former stepfather to apologize for being so nasty toward him during the divorce scandal. And I felt that would be my mother's wish: that her children would make peace with the past and be able to move forward, so I had no objections to these calls and conversations. Nor am I opposed to the fact that the two of them still see each other, over a year and a half later, recovering their lost friendship. That afternoon, Melele took him to the amusement park. I chose not to go. It was about reuniting Esteban and Johnny, not Esteban and Chiquis. Some months later, Esteban would break his silence and send me a text to say hello. I was happy to hear from him and replied back warmly, but to this day we have yet to meet in person, and we don't have any plans to do so. I know that someday our paths will cross again, but I'll leave it up to fate to decide when and where. This is another one of those stories that is better left without an ending.

And speaking of endings, I had other, more important battles that I needed to resolve. I had to show the world that I would not crack. That Jenni's daughter had inherited the balls to leave nothing half done. I went back to the studio and recorded my second song, "Esa No Soy Yo." The lyrics fit like a glove. I wrote it with Julio Reyes, who is also my vocal coach and close friend, and it was about many things, some personal and some not so personal. It was the perfect song to put an end to "poor Chiquis" and kick off my big moment. This one wasn't dedicated to my mother, but she was very close to my heart while I wrote and recorded it. The premier would be onstage at the Univision Youth Awards.

"Are you sure about that, Chiquis?" my publicist, Iris, asked. "Remember that's a very prestigious award show. It's broadcast in several countries, and all eyes will be on you."

"I'm ready, love. I couldn't care less what they might say. And remember what my momma always said: 'Don't worry about bad things being said about you. The time to worry is when they're not talking about you at all.'"

"You're right. Damn the haters! You are not alone."

That's how it was. I was not alone. I didn't feel it for a second, even when I got to Miami. During rehearsals, my mother was with me. When I was trying on the dress that was designed for me by the Estrada twins, she was there to give her approval. When the fans along the red carpet were yelling, "You look just like your mom!" I said, "Of course! I always do, no matter what I'm wearing. Telling me I look like her is the biggest compliment!"

That night, I could hear the crowd cheering from the dressing room. Great performers were already heading onto the stage, which promised to be the most anticipated event of the summer. My team was nervous, but ready to take the stage and succeed. We brought Javier de la Rosa from Mexico just to do my makeup. Javier was a friend of our dear Jacob, and they both had a similar style of work. Javier talked a lot about Jacob while he transformed me for my performance, and I felt him there, with us, as was my mother, arguing about the eyelashes or what lip gloss to use, and telling jokes. Meanwhile, my manager, Guillermo Rosas, was coming and going, giving orders to Iris and answering calls. We were all there, just like the old times!

"Chiquis to the stage! Chiquis to the stage!" they shouted from down the hall. It was time. Jose Manuel Martínez, el Torito, my good friend and assistant, took my hand and led me to the seat where I would be lifted by a crane to the very top of the auditorium.

Guillermo gave me one last hug and said, "Chiquis, we've been together for nearly two years now, and no matter what happens tonight, we're going to stay together."

I smiled with infinite gratitude. And as I was being lifted up through the air, I heard Torito shouting after me: "You're awesome, and everyone who ever talked shit about you is gonna have to shut up!"

Ah, my faithful Torito . . .

Being up there, suspended in the air over the impressive

Bank United Center, with thousands of people packing the place, I heard my mother's voice, strong and clear in my head: "We got this. Everything's under control." It was the first time I'd heard it since the Graduation! Then the crane began to operate, lowering me down into the center of the stage, and when the camera focused on me, I took a deep breath. I grabbed the microphone with the same strength that I used when I held on to my mother during those bike rides as a child. "Just a little step . . . Slower . . . A little louder . . ." My mother's voice was guiding me. "Another little step . . . To the right . . . Head up . . ." She was coaching me through every move. Feeling neither fear nor nerves, I started to enjoy my moment. "Take a step . . . Wait for it . . . Now hit it!" And with that voice in my heart, I belted out the final verse:

But you got it twisted
I'm not that girl
I'm not that girl . . .

And that's when I shouted, "*Gracias!* I love you! I love you all!"

Two producers helped me down the difficult stairs, and the first one to meet me at the foot of the stage was Guillermo with a look of total bliss on his face.

"You fucking rocked it!" he said, totally thrilled.

"You did it! You did it, baby!" Iris congratulated me, running up to give me one of her massive hugs.

Everyone was waiting for me in the dressing room: my siblings, Dayanna, my tío Juan, my tía Rosie. Everyone united, laughing and celebrating a family victory. Just the way my mother would have wanted it. We were all there, including her, without distances, without fear, without misunderstandings. Together and at peace.

242

As I was removing my makeup in front of the mirror—and while the rest of the group was laughing and raving—I thought to myself, *I promise you, Momma, that this year I'll change my name. That will be my gift to you. No more Marín. My driver's license will say Janney Rivera. Yes, that's me.*

26.
DON'T WORRY

Here it is, Chiquis. I think it came," Melele said, holding in her hand one of those manila envelopes that normally contain documents.

"No way!" I tore into it right away, while Jenicka smiled and Johnny was looking on impatiently. "It's a present from Mom: approved!"

"Congratulations," my Johnny said, his voice very serious. "You just gave birth to a couple of teenagers. You're a hot mom."

Waving the papers in the air, we had a group hug. Even Melele joined in. The process of taking over custody of the kids, which had started months before, was now final. A simple little term, but with so much significance attached to it: I had always been their legal guardian.

A few days after the custody papers came, my tía Rosie decided it was time to start her new life as well. For the time being, she would move in with Grandma Rosa before deciding whether to look for a new house or stay at the one in Lakewood.

The morning of her move, I found a note on the fridge:

Thank you for sharing your home with us, and for always making us feel welcome here. This isn't good-bye, because we'll see you tomorrow. We're family.

My eyes filled with tears. Rosie and I shared pains and sorrows together when we were kids, but it was nothing compared with what we'd been through in the past two years. It hadn't been an easy road for any of us. And now it was coming to an end.

I ran out to find her, and I caught her just as she was loading the last of her suitcases into the trunk of her car. Her husband and her two beautiful girls were waiting for her.

"My work here is done. Don't be sad, Chiquis. We always knew it was only temporary."

"Yes, but I don't want you leaving thinking that we ran you out or something."

"No, it's all good. The most important thing is that we all do what your mom would have wanted. It doesn't matter what she wrote in her will. We both know she wanted you to stay with the kids. There's no doubt about that."

"Thank you, tía. This will always be your home too."

"And it will always be the home of Jenni and Chiquis."

And with a deeply felt "I love you," we bid farewell to that stage of our lives.

When the car had disappeared down the hill, I went back inside the house and shut the enormous doors with the wrought iron monogram that read JR.

"Now I'm the one telling you, Momma: don't worry. Your family and your home are all good. I got this."

YOU don't worry.

EPILOGUE

The last lesson my momma taught me is one that gave me my masters degree from the university of LIFE. She taught me not to depend on anyone, because even our shadows disappear in the darkness. I strongly believe that she subconsciously left me two months before graduating to heaven so that I could learn to stand on my own two feet and be strong enough for my siblings. Thus, I was left two steps ahead in the grieving process for a reason. All the pain and sometimes anger generated fire in my soul forcing me to press forward, especially in all of 2013. I didn't understand it then, but now I'm ready and willing to earn my doctorate degree as I wait to graduate from this world. The world may be tough, but I'm tougher. Now, more than ever know that instead of running from the pain, I was built to embrace it, because every experience is an opportunity to learn something new about ourselves and together, grow from it. After all, pain is only a pass to mental and spiritual promotion. If you're wise enough to receive it, you'll gain it. Life is a big mess, but that's the beeUty of it. . . We're meant to evolve for the better good. #BeeWise #QueenBee

Much has happened to me in my twenty-nine years on this earth. Some of it has been wonderful, some of it has been terrible, some of it has been hard to comprehend. And forgiveness was not my first instinct when life was tragic or confusing. But today I can finally say that I hold no resentment toward anyone or any circumstance that has happened to me. I accept with grace all that occurred during my childhood at the hands of those who were truly troubled. I accept with grace all that has happened since October 2012 and the decisions that my mom made. I accept with faith and humility the path that God has put me on since I first entered this world; I may not always understand it, but I feel free and content with the plan that He has for my life.

Now, as I finish these pages, I'm reminded of the fact that forgiveness should always be a two-lane road. So I want to apologize to those whom I've already forgiven in due course, but to whom I haven't officially offered my own apologies for the pain I caused them.

The first one I would like to apologize to is my grandma Rosa. Throughout this whole family drama, I feel that we lost sight of you, Grandma, and that we didn't listen to you as we should have. You gave us so much advice, and yet we always seemed to get it wrong! You, Grandma, have the wisdom life and your enormous love of God have given you. Forgive me, also, for not calling or visiting you more often, and for not giving you the attention you deserve. After all, you were my first mom, the one who gave me my first real home, and, of course, all those beans.

Forgive me, Tío Juan and Tía Rosie, for pushing you out of my life. I was so focused on my own pain that I lost sight of the fact that you also lost someone: your sister. I know that everything you did during those two years was for our own good, and I apologize for not understanding it at the time, when I was wallowing in my own sorrow. Pain can sometimes make you selfish. I'm sorry.

And I need to extend more forgiveness to another guy who has also been like a father to me. How could I ever forget those bags of crispy taquitos you brought me each day just to see me smile when you walked in the door of the house on Ellis Street? My dear tío Lupe, even as I write these words, and while we have a conversation pending and many issues to resolve, I want you to know that I'm forgiving you a little bit more with every passing day. There were some things you did the week we lost my mother that I didn't like, and during the past two years, you've distanced yourself from us a lot. But remember that the Rivera family is a very lucky one: we can fight however much we want, but the love that unites us is stronger than a thousand arguments and disagreements. We've hurt ourselves enough. I think you had time to reconcile with my mother during those four weeks before she left us. But I didn't. Let's not repeat that. Let's not tempt fate. I'm here with my phone in hand, waiting for you to call so that I can forgive you, and so you can forgive me.

To my beautiful sister Jacqie, I'm sorry because I don't tell you I love you as often as I did when we were little. I never meant to make you feel excluded. Forgive me, because being the second child isn't easy. Growing up as number two forced you to follow my orders and inherit my sneakers. And for me, being the first meant I grew up thinking I knew it all. That's the arrogance of an older sister. But I want you to know that, in my heart, you will always be MY number one, because you were the first sister that God gave me, and our history together is filled with pages that will never fade. Forgive me, Jacquelin.

And, finally, I want to apologize to that little girl who liked to sing, the one who loved going to the swap meet every Saturday with her grandparents. To the girl who lives inside of me. With everything that was going on, I forgot about you and neglected to give you the love and time that you needed. I got lost in trying to please the world, and I forgot to pamper you the way you deserve.

But it's never too late, and you're still that same little girl in my heart. And so I promise you that, from this day forward, I'll take a moment to buy you a *chocolate caliente* and one of those *bolillos* before the swap meet closes, and I'll sit down on a bench with you and take the time to enjoy them.

If you can forgive me, my little companion, you'll be giving me wings to fly freely. Because in my short but intense life, I've learned a couple things, and the most important one of all is that only through forgiveness can we achieve true FREEDOM.

A LETTER TO MY MOTHER

Dear Momma,

It feels like forever since the last time I wrote you a letter, and today it breaks my heart to know that I will never write another Mother's Day card. I can't even explain the pain in my heart I feel every morning from missing you; sometimes I can't catch my breath from how much it hurts. I have been upset at the world, at God, at you, at myself and at life in general for taking you away so quickly without an explanation, without a final good-bye. My faith has been tested. Losing you without talking to you one more time was unbearable, as was dealing with the aftermath.

I was somehow left alone to figure out how to navigate the gossip that pervaded my life. I needed you, Momma, and didn't know how to face the world without your ever-present protection. You always handled the media so well. I didn't know what to do, and I doubted myself until the day I decided to write this book. At first, writing it was a way of telling my side of the story, but as time passed, I realized that this book was so much more. This is my tribute to you. I decided to use these pages to heal me from the inside. It has truly been a journey to *FORGIVENESS*.

Momma, we had a beautiful love story. Our bond, and all we

encountered in life together, was by many standards simply crazy, but you taught me to face the tornado head-on. And today I feel that you stand with me and my siblings every day.

I am writing this letter on my flight back home from Las Vegas. I can't help but think of you each time I fly, especially after a day like today. The autograph signing was such a success, the people there were so loving and affectionate toward me . . . and I have no one else to thank but you and God.

Thank you for all your hard work.

Thank you for never giving up and teaching me to be a warrior, just like you.

Thank you for making me a strong and independent woman.

Thank you for being so hard on me sometimes.

Thank you for your strong and meaningful life lessons.

Thank you for singing that last song to me.

Thank you for being the BEST, the greatest mom a girl could have.

Momma:

Forgive me for not appreciating your lessons.

Forgive me for being, at times, critical and hard on you too.

Forgive me for not saying I love you often enough.

It sucks that we don't appreciate what we have in the palm of our hands until it's gone. Until it's no longer in our reach.

I miss you so damn much.

I confess there have been days when I have asked God to take me with you. I yearn for your protective hugs that always made me feel as if I belonged somewhere. But I quickly recall your words, "Don't bitch out, Chiquis." Those words will always remind me to be the strong woman you raised. I promise you, Momma, that I will remain standing. Not only for the kids and myself, but for the world, because I remember our plan. I won't give up until, through hard work, I get us there.

Momma, I also need you to know that I truly forgive you. I know you didn't mean to leave me with a mess or to hurt me in any way. I know that in your heart you never believed I was capable of betraying you. I am sure we would have talked and figured it all out. But a bad twist of fate got ahead of us and didn't give us the time. I know you know the truth, and that gives me peace.

Mommy, the plane is now descending and I gotta get off and check on our babies. But before I do, I want you to know that you are and will always be the love of my life. The sole owner of my heart. *Eres mi todo*. And I can't wait until the day God lets me see you again.

I love you from here to Heaven, momma bear!

♥

Your big princess, Quismin!

And once the storm is over, you won't remember how you made it through, how you managed to survive. You won't even be sure, whether the storm is really over. But one thing is certain. When you come out of the storm, you won't be the same person who walked in. That's what this storm's all about.

—HARUKI MURAKAMI, *KAFKA ON THE SHORE*

ACKNOWLEDGMENTS

I would like to thank my momma, for being my rock, my mentor and my daily inspiration. Without you, this book wouldn't exist. I love you to infinity and beyond!

Thank you to my brothers and sisters—Jacqie, Mikey, Jenicka and Johnny—for being my strength on a daily basis, especially after December 9. Thanks for giving me your unconditional love and teaching me to be a stronger woman. You are the owner of my heart.

To *mis abuelitos*, Doña Rosa and Don Pedro Rivera, the pillars of our family. Thank you for your efforts, sacrifice and dedication to our family. *Gracias por su amor y su ejemplo a seguir. Los amo abuelitos.*

Thank you, Tío Juan, the only real father figure I've had, for your advice, love, and protection. For defending me when no one else did, but, mainly, thank you for loving me, flaws and all. I love you.

To my wonderful cousin Karina, thank you for having my back no matter what, since we were little girls who swam in your pool for hours at a time! Thank you for making me laugh and supporting my every move. Thank you for simply being YOU.

To my great friends Gerald Gamble, Julie Anguiano, Ellen

Mariona, Briana Hauser and Yadira Quinonez, thank you for being by my side before the storm and staying by my side during it and now that the storm has passed. Thank you for loving, accepting, and caring about my well-being no matter what my circumstances have been. I love and appreciate each one of you VERY much.

To my best friend, Dayanna Soto (Quintero), my soul sister, thank you for being there with me through the hardest moments of my life and believing in me when I didn't believe in myself. Thanks for your loyalty and friendship, but I am even more grateful for our endless conversations of substance and silliness. I love you, sister.

A huge thank you to my AMAZING team: my manager, Guillermo Rosas, at Sixth House; my publicist, Iris Corral; Jose Manuel Martinez (El Torito); Julio Reyes, my vocal coach; and Neomi Valdivia and everybody at Sixth House for working hard for my musical career. Thank you for your unconditional support, advice and honesty. But mostly thank you for believing in me and in my vision.

To my #bossbeenation, my fans and the people who support my career no matter what BS has been said or written about me. Thank you for loving me unconditionally with no expectations or limits, but mainly, thank you for giving me the opportunity to show you all who I really am. For opening your hearts and allowing yourselves to get to know me a little better. I heart you all. I'm so blessed to have your support.

Thanks to María García, who listened to me like a sister. We walked together through the journey of writing a book. Thank you for your hard work. Are you ready for book number two?

Thanks to the other angel in my life who has guided me, protected me and helped me become a wiser and stronger woman. No matter what the future holds, I will always #beegrateful. I love you, my #BBN27.

Thank you to all my family and friends who may not have been mentioned here, but who are equally as important and have in some way played a HUGE part in my personal and professional growth. I love you ALL.

This journey would not have been possible without the help of some wonderful people at Atria Books: my publisher, Judith Curr, and my dear editor, Johanna Castillo, along with the entire team at Atria Books in New York. Thank you for believing in my story.

DO YOU NEED HELP?

You're not alone. You are not alone.

Visit: www.bossbeenation.net

Join our online beehive and get involved with other readers of *FORGIVENESS*.

Ask questions.
Offer advice.
Find information.
Share your opinions.
And everything is completely anonymous.

Experts and other survivors of abuse, bullying and domestic violence will be there at bossbeenation to help.

Here are some other places where survivors of abuse can find the support they need, and they speak Spanish too:

National Sexual Assault Hotline
1-800-656-HOPE

DO YOU NEED HELP?

Rape Abuse & Incest National Network
https://www.rainn.org

Stop Bullying
http://www.stopbullying.gov

National Domestic Violence Hotline
1-800-799-7233
http://www.thehotline.org